DATE DUE

OCT 1 9 2006			

Crimes Against Humanity

CRIME, JUSTICE, AND PUNISHMENT

Crimes Against Humanity

Neil Chippendale

Austin Sarat, GENERAL EDITOR

CHELSEA HOUSE PUBLISHERS
Philadelphia

Frontispiece: *Reviewing the carnage at this massacre site in Kosovo, an observer may wonder how something like this could be allowed. These murders become more disturbing with the realization that they were sanctioned by the government as part of a campaign to wipe out ethnic Albanians in the small eastern European province.*

Chelsea House Publishers

Editor in Chief Stephen Reginald
Production Manager Pamela Loos
Art Director Sara Davis
Director of Photography Judy L. Hasday
Managing Editor James D. Gallagher
Senior Production Editor J. Christopher Higgins

Staff for CRIMES AGAINST HUMANITY

Associate Art Director/Designer Takeshi Takahashi
Picture Researcher Patricia Burns
Cover Illustrator Emiliano Begnardi

First Printing

1 3 5 7 9 8 6 4 2

The Chelsea House World Wide Web address is
http://www.chelseahouse.com

Library of Congress Cataloging-in-Publication Data

Chippendale, Neil.
Crimes against humanity / Neil Chippendale
    p.   cm. — (Crime, justice and punishment)
Includes bibliographical references and index.
Summary: Discusses incidents of various crimes against
humanity, including particular war crimes and acts of geno-
cide, and ways to prevent these atrocities.

ISBN 0-7910-4254-5 (hc)

1. Crimes against humanity—Juvenile literature. 2. War
crimes—Juvenile literature. 3. Genocide—Juvenile literature. [1. Crimes against humanity. 2. War crimes. 3.
Genocide.] I. Title: At head of title: Crime, Justice, and
punishment. II. Title. III. Series.

K5301.C48 2000
341.6'9—dc21

Contents

CRIME, JUSTICE, AND PUNISHMENT

CAPITAL PUNISHMENT

CHILDREN, VIOLENCE, AND MURDER

CLASSIC CONS AND SWINDLES

CRIMES AGAINST CHILDREN:
CHILD ABUSE AND NEGLECT

CRIMES AGAINST HUMANITY

CYBER CRIMES

DEFENSE LAWYERS

DRUGS, CRIME,
AND CRIMINAL JUSTICE

THE DUTY TO RESCUE

ESPIONAGE AND TREASON

THE FBI

THE FBI'S MOST WANTED

FORENSIC SCIENCE

GANGS AND CRIME

THE GRAND JURY

GREAT PROSECUTIONS

GREAT ROBBERIES

GUNS, CRIME, AND
THE SECOND AMENDMENT

HATE CRIMES

HIGH CRIMES AND MISDEMEANORS:
THE IMPEACHMENT PROCESS

INFAMOUS TRIALS

THE INSANITY DEFENSE

JUDGES AND SENTENCING

THE JURY SYSTEM

JUVENILE CRIME

MAJOR UNSOLVED CRIMES

ORGANIZED CRIME

PRISONS

PRIVATE INVESTIGATORS
AND BOUNTY HUNTERS

PUNISHMENT AND REHABILITATION

RACE, CRIME, AND PUNISHMENT

REVENGE AND RETRIBUTION

RIGHTS OF THE ACCUSED

SERIAL MURDER

TERRORISM

VICTIMS AND VICTIMS' RIGHTS

WHITE-COLLAR CRIME

Fears and Fascinations:

An Introduction to Crime, Justice, and Punishment

By Austin Sarat

We live with crime and images of crime all around us. Crime evokes in most of us a deep aversion, a feeling of profound vulnerability, but it also evokes an equally deep fascination. Today, in major American cities the fear of crime is a major fact of life, some would say a disproportionate response to the realities of crime. Yet the fear of crime is real, palpable in the quickened steps and furtive glances of people walking down darkened streets. At the same time, we eagerly follow crime stories on television and in movies. We watch with a "who done it" curiosity, eager to see the illicit deed done, the investigation undertaken, the miscreant brought to justice and given his just deserts. On the streets the presence of crime is a reminder of our own vulnerability and the precariousness of our taken-for-granted rights and freedoms. On television and in the movies the crime story gives us a chance to probe our own darker motives, to ask "Is there a criminal within?" as well as to feel the collective satisfaction of seeing justice done.

7

Fear and fascination, these two poles of our engagement with crime, are, of course, only part of the story. Crime is, after all, a major social and legal problem, not just an issue of our individual psychology. Politicians today use our fear of, and fascination with, crime for political advantage. How we respond to crime, as well as to the political uses of the crime issue, tells us a lot about who we are as a people as well as what we value and what we tolerate. Is our response compassionate or severe? Do we seek to understand or to punish, to enact an angry vengeance or to rehabilitate and welcome the criminal back into our midst? The CRIME, JUSTICE, AND PUNISHMENT series is designed to explore these themes, to ask why we are fearful and fascinated, to probe the meanings and motivations of crimes and criminals and of our responses to them, and, finally, to ask what we can learn about ourselves and the society in which we live by examining our responses to crime.

Crime is always a challenge to the prevailing normative order and a test of the values and commitments of law-abiding people. It is sometimes a Raskolnikov-like act of defiance, an assertion of the unwillingness of some to live according to the rules of conduct laid out by organized society. In this sense, crime marks the limits of the law and reminds us of law's all-too-regular failures. Yet sometimes there is more desperation than defiance in criminal acts; sometimes they signal a deep pathology or need in the criminal. To confront crime is thus also to come face-to-face with the reality of social difference, of class privilege and extreme deprivation, of race and racism, of children neglected, abandoned, or abused whose response is to enact on others what they have experienced themselves. And occasionally crime, or what is labeled a criminal act, represents a call for justice, an appeal to a higher moral order against the inadequacies of existing law.

Figuring out the meaning of crime and the motivations of criminals and whether crime arises from defiance, desperation, or the appeal for justice is never an easy task. The motivations and meanings of crime are as varied as are the persons who engage in criminal conduct. They are as mysterious as any of the mysteries of the human soul. Yet the desire to know the secrets of crime and the criminal is a strong one, for in that knowledge may lie one step on the road to protection, if not an assurance of one's own personal safety. Nonetheless, as strong as that desire may be, there is no available technology that can allow us to know the whys of crime with much confidence, let alone a scientific certainty. We can, however, capture something about crime by studying the defiance, desperation, and quest for justice that may be associated with it. Books in the CRIME, JUSTICE, AND PUNISHMENT series will take up that challenge. They tell stories of crime and criminals, some famous, most not, some glamorous and exciting, most mundane and commonplace.

This series will, in addition, take a sober look at American criminal justice, at the procedures through which we investigate crimes and identify criminals, at the institutions in which innocence or guilt is determined. In these procedures and institutions we confront the thrill of the chase as well as the challenge of protecting the rights of those who defy our laws. It is through the efficiency and dedication of law enforcement that we might capture the criminal; it is in the rare instances of their corruption or brutality that we feel perhaps our deepest betrayal. Police, prosecutors, defense lawyers, judges, and jurors administer criminal justice and in their daily actions give substance to the guarantees of the Bill of Rights. What is an adversarial system of justice? How does it work? Why do we have it? Books in the CRIME, JUSTICE, AND PUNISHMENT series will examine the thrill of the chase as we seek to capture the criminal. They will also reveal the drama and majesty of the criminal trial as well as the day-to-day reality of a criminal justice system in which trials are the exception and negotiated pleas of guilty are the rule.

When the trial is over or the plea has been entered, when we have separated the innocent from the guilty, the moment of punishment has arrived. The injunction to punish the guilty, to respond to pain inflicted by inflicting pain, is as old as civilization itself. "An eye for an eye and a tooth for a tooth" is a biblical reminder that punishment must measure pain for pain. But our response to the criminal must be better than and different from the crime itself. The biblical admonition, along with the constitutional prohibition of "cruel and unusual punishment," signals that we seek to punish justly and to be just not only in the determination of who can and should be punished, but in how we punish as well. But neither reminder tells us what to do with the wrongdoer. Do we rape the rapist, or burn the home of the arsonist? Surely justice and decency say no. But, if not, then how can and should we punish? In a world in which punishment is neither identical to the crime nor an automatic response to it, choices must be made and we must make them. Books in the CRIME, JUSTICE, AND PUNISHMENT series will examine those choices and the practices, and politics, of punishment. How do we punish and why do we punish as we do? What can we learn about the rationality and appropriateness of today's responses to crime by examining our past and its responses? What works? Is there, and can there be, a just measure of pain?

CRIME, JUSTICE, AND PUNISHMENT brings together books on some of the great themes of human social life. The books in this series capture our fear and fascination with crime and examine our responses to it. They remind us of the deadly seriousness of these subjects. They bring together themes in law, literature, and popular culture to challenge us to think again, to think anew, about subjects that go to the heart of who we are and how we can and will live together.

*   *   *   *   *

The twentieth century may well be remembered for many things. But surely among the most gruesome memories will be recollections of mass extermination, genocide, Holocaust. Collectively we have come to call these barbarous acts crimes against humanity. Typically these are acts directed against persons because of their membership in certain groups—their race, ethnicity, nationality. Most often these crimes are committed by governments or states in the name of national purpose or collective revenge. These crimes raise vexing questions going not only to the nature of human social conduct, but also to the nature and function of law. How can an act that is legal within a particular nation be deemed illegal by forces beyond its borders?

This book engages with those questions by taking us through both the atrocities that were so characteristic of the twentieth century, and of the varying legal responses to them. It provides a vivid examination of the forces propelling crimes against humanity and the evolving legal responses. It reminds us that at the start of the new century we must be vigilant not to think that we have adequately understood these crimes or that we have figured out what a just response to them can be.

Kosovo

In 1389, on the broad plain surrounding the city of Pristina, Kosovo, the Serbian Prince Lazar and his army fought to the death against the far stronger army of the Muslim Ottoman Empire. In time the Battle of Kosovo Polje came to symbolize the fierce pride and fearlessness of the Serbian nation. To the Serbs Kosovo is holy ground, the birthplace of their nation, even though they did not regain control of this plain and the surrounding mountains until the peace settlement of 1919 that ended World War I and formed the Republic of Yugoslavia.

Six hundred years after the Battle of Kosovo Polje, a politician from the Yugoslavian republic of Serbia

Coffins draped with Albanian flags are carried through Racak, Kosovo, during a funeral procession. The dead were more than 40 ethnic Albanian citizens who had been murdered by Serbian forces on January 15, 1999. The Racak massacre was part of a larger campaign of terror instituted by the Serbs in an attempt to rid Kosovo of its ethnic Albanian majority.

named Slobodan Milosevic built his career on issues regarding Kosovo. Serbian residents of Kosovo felt that they were being oppressed by an unfriendly Albanian majority that made up 90 percent of the province's population. The Kosovar Serbs were delighted when Milosevic, in a 1987 speech, told them that they would never be beaten again. When he became president of Yugoslavia, Milosevic placed Kosovo, an independent province of the Republic of Serbia, under the central government's control.

Non-Serbian people throughout Yugoslavia did not care for Milosevic's iron rule. Slovenia and Croatia, two other Yugoslav republics, fought successfully for independence from the central government. Later a bloody war was fought in the Yugoslavian republic of Bosnia as Milosevic sought to maintain control there. In 1999, armed warfare returned to Kosovo as Milosevic sent government troops to suppress the province's ethnic majority—Albanians who, like the Croats, Slovenians, and Bosnians before them, also wished to separate from Yugoslavia. It was not until the intervention of the North Atlantic Treaty Organization (NATO), a military alliance of European nations and the United States, that Serbian troops left Kosovo. After an intense NATO aerial bombardment in the winter and spring of 1999, Milosevic was forced to withdraw his troops and allow NATO peacekeepers to occupy the province.

The stories from Kosovo—tales of massacres, rapes, executions, and random killings—are gruesome. Before the start of NATO air strikes, Milosevic used terror and violence in an attempt to force more than 600,000 Kosovar Albanians from their homes. In one example of this violence, 45 ethnic Albanians were murdered by Serbian paramilitary forces in the village of Racak on January 15, 1999. The bullet-riddled bodies of men, women, and children were found strewn in gullies, some shot through the head. The day after the NATO

air strikes started in March, the violence against Albanians escalated. Sixty-four men, women, and children living in the village of Bela Crvka were murdered along the bank of the Belleh River. In Dakovica, at least 350 people are believed to have been murdered during a systematic sweep of Kosovar Albanian neighborhoods. Near Cikatovo, Serbian paramilitary forces executed 70 to 80 male prisoners. In Velika Krusa, 20 villagers were murdered and their bodies burned. Additional mass grave sites are being discovered all over Kosovo, and authorities of the United Nations think that over 10,000 victims will eventually be discovered.

In June 1999, Yugoslav President Slobodan Milosevic became the first sitting head of state to be indicted for crimes against humanity. Milosevic and four aides were indicted by the United Nations' International

Serbian president Slobodan Milosevic speaks at a press conference outside the United Nations. Milosevic was the architect of genocidal violence in both Kosovo and the former Yugoslav republic of Bosnia. In 1999 he became the first sitting head of state to be indicted for crimes against humanity.

Mass murders, such as this one of ethnic Albanian Kosovars by Serb forces, are typically considered crimes against humanity. This can be defined as an atrocity (for example, murder or enslavement) that is committed by the government of a country against an entire population or part of a population of its citizens.

Criminal Tribunal, which charged them as responsible for the persecution, deportation, and murder of hundreds of thousands of ethnic Albanians. The indictment alleged that Milosevic and his aides "planned, instigated, ordered, committed or otherwise ordered and abetted" a campaign against Albanians in Kosovo. Forces commanded by Milosevic and others "engaged in a well planned and coordinated campaign of destruction of property owned by Kosovo Albanian civilians. Towns and villages have been shelled; homes, farms and businesses burned; and personal property destroyed," the indictment claims, stating that "the unlawful deportation and forcible transfer of thousands of Kosovo Albanians from their homes involved well planned and coordinated efforts by the leaders of the Federal Republic of Yugoslavia and Serbia."

However, Milosevic may never face prosecution for his crimes against humanity. Although he faces the threat of immediate arrest if he leaves his own country, it is unlikely that the United States or NATO will ever invade Serbia to try to arrest him. The best hope is that a new government will come to power in Yugoslavia one day, and will turn Milosevic over for a trial by the International Criminal Tribunal.

❧   ❧   ❧

Although the terms "war crimes" and "crimes against humanity" are often used synonymously, they do not necessarily mean the same thing. War crimes are violations of the international laws of war, which are outlined in both written treaties and unwritten customs. The laws of war limit the type of violence that is permissible in war, and regulate the extent of that violence against the armies and civilians of other nations. For example, the mistreatment of prisoners of war, or of the population of a captured territory, would violate the laws of war, thus constituting a war crime.

A crime against humanity is defined as an atrocity, such as extermination or enslavement, against an entire population or part of a population. Instead of being committed against enemy soldiers or citizens, however, this atrocity is often directed by the government of a country toward its own citizens, for whom the laws and customs of war provide no protection. And although the leaders who order and direct these actions may state their reasons, typically these reasons are without merit. In most cases members of the group that is being persecuted are considered to be guilty just because they are members of that group.

What often distinguishes crimes against humanity

are the extraordinary brutality employed to commit these crimes, and the persecution and extermination of whole peoples that far exceed the definition of war crimes in the traditional sense. The actions committed by Nazi Germany in the 1930s and 1940s are a perfect example of crimes against humanity. The Nazis engaged in a policy of deliberate, systematic extermination of all Jews, today known as the Holocaust. In addition, the Nazis also relentlessly persecuted, enslaved, and murdered Roman Catholics, Gypsies, Slavs, Poles, homosexuals, the mentally ill, the handicapped, and political dissidents. More than 6 million people, most of them Jews, died in the Holocaust. The Nazi leaders who were in charge of the government agencies that hunted down, arrested, and transported millions of innocent people to their deaths in concentration camps, were guilty of crimes against humanity.

The right of nations to intervene in the internal affairs of another nation for humanitarian reasons has been considered part of international law since before the Second World War. However, as the full extent of Nazi Germany's offenses became clearer, the Allies realized that no precedent existed in international law for the prosecution of war criminals for crimes against humanity. Although special courts had been set up in the past, none had obtained official international recognition. The Allied powers were determined to prosecute war criminals on sound legal procedures. The Moscow Declaration of 1945, an agreement between the United States, England, France, and the USSR, established the International Military Tribunal, which tried the major war criminals of World War II and included a definition of crimes against humanity as follows:

> Murder, extermination, enslavement, deportation and other inhumane acts committed against any civilian population before or during the war, or persecutions on political, racial or religious grounds of execution of or in conjunction with any crime within the jurisdiction of the

Tribunal, whether or not in violation of the domestic laws of the country where perpetrated.

This Tribunal established crimes against humanity as offenses under international law, just as war crimes had been previously established. A later convention would also establish genocide—the deliberate and systematic destruction of a racial, political, or cultural group—as a special crime against humanity that could also be a war crime.

Since the end of the Cold War there has been an increase in atrocities and crimes against humanity. The United Nations and the international community has

Thousands of refugees fled Kosovo for neighboring Albania as Milosevic and his Serb forces stepped up their attacks in 1999. Worldwide, the incidence of crimes against humanity appears to be on the rise.

slowly been taking on the responsibility for justice through the use of temporary international criminal tribunals. Tribunals have been created by the United Nations Security Council to prosecute offenders like Milosevic, as well as government officials in other countries where crimes against humanity have been committed. One of these countries is the African nation of Rwanda, where as many as one million people may have been massacred during a violent uprising between April and June 1994.

The ultimate weapon of international judicial intervention would be a permanent International Criminal Court (ICC) that would establish and enforce an international rule of law that national governments and their leaders must obey. The Nuremberg and Tokyo war crimes tribunals that followed the Second World War inspired serious efforts to create an ICC. But those efforts soon became bogged down with the endless task of selecting and defining the crimes that would form the jurisdiction of the court. It took the United Nations almost two decades to reach a definition for the crime of aggression, and even that has proven too imprecise. And the protracted effort to create a Code of Crimes Against the Peace and Security of Mankind, which would define crimes indictable by an international criminal court, continues within the U.N.'s International Law Commission.

Fifty years of difficulty notwithstanding, the proposal for a permanent tribunal is gaining ground. Governments recognize that international crimes that threaten peace and security are on the rise.

The final weapon of enforcement requires patience by all who are frustrated by the paucity of indicted individuals in the tribunal's custody to date. Years of work will be necessary to apprehend and bring to justice all those indicted by both the Yugoslav tribunal (over 50 to date) and the Rwanda tribunal (the ringleaders of the program of genocide carried out in this African country in the mid-1990s may number more than 100). But that is the nature of prosecuting crimes against humanity. The post–World War II experience with Nazi war criminals shows how long and difficult it can be to track down and bring to justice those who have committed these atrocities.

THE "RULE OF WAR" AND WAR CRIMES

For thousands of years, both written and unwritten customs have regulated the waging of war. Today, these "laws of war" are set forth in numerous treaties, most notably the Hague conferences of 1899 and 1907, which established rules for conducting land and naval warfare as part of international law, and the Geneva conventions, which set forth guidelines for the treatment of civilians and prisoners during wartime.

The idea of "laws of war" developed along with civilization. Originally, the victorious army could, and did, act however barbarically it wished. But even thousands of years ago, though common practices included killing or enslaving conquered people, there were guidelines for the use of violence. For example, the biblical book of Deuteronomy gave the Israelites the following guidance for warfare:

> When you march up to attack a city, first offer it terms of peace. If it agrees to your terms of peace and opens its

gates to you, all the people to be found in it shall serve you in forced labor. But if it refuses to make peace with you and instead offers you battle, lay siege to it, and when the Lord, your God, delivers it into your hand, put every male in it to the sword; but all the women and children and livestock and all else in it that is worth plundering you may take as your booty. . . .

That is how you shall deal with any city at a considerable distance from you, which does not belong to the peoples of [Canaan]. But in the cities of [Canaan], you shall not leave a single soul alive.

Deuteronomy also told the Israelites that while they were besieging a city, they could not cut down the fruit trees that surround it. "You may eat their fruit, but . . . . after all, are the trees of the field men, that they should be included in your siege?"

It was common for ancient Greeks to commit various cruelties during war: sacrifices to appease the gods, and slaughter or enslavement of surrendered enemy soldiers or the populations of captured towns. Enslavement was a common, and accepted, fate of the vanquished. When the Greeks were finally victorious in their 10-year war against the Trojans, as described in Homer's *Iliad* and Virgil's *Aeneid*, they destroyed the city and took many of its inhabitants as slaves, and the Bible describes how the Israelites were eventually defeated and enslaved by the Babylonians. It was also common for soldiers to capture, rather than kill, their enemies if they were promised a ransom for their safe return. Captured soldiers could also be enslaved, or could be exchanged for soldiers who had been captured by the other side.

While the treatment of prisoners seems brutal by today's standards, the rules of war were strictly observed, and those who violated them faced fierce reprisals. When the Trojan hero Hector is mortally wounded in the *Iliad*, he asks his enemy Achilles to allow his body to be ransomed by his parents, a standard practice of the time. However, the Trojan had

killed Achilles's closest friend, and the angry Greek warrior desecrates Hector's corpse by allowing the other Greeks to stab it numerous times, then tying it to the back of his chariot and dragging it around his friend's funeral pyre. Because this behavior goes against the customs of warfare as set down by the Greek gods, Achilles eventually is ordered by Hermes, messenger of the gods, to surrender the corpse to Hector's parents.

The Romans followed many of the same rules of war; during Julius Caesar's second invasion of Gaul, he enslaved 33,000 Belgians that his forces had captured. However, Romans also argued for leniency toward defeated foes. A group of Roman philosophers, known

From the scaffold, Pope Urban II proclaims the first crusade, an effort by Christian knights to take back the Holy Land from the Muslims living there in the 11th century. The crusades were brutal, bloody affairs; neither side showed mercy.

Scottish patriot William Wallace (top) was a thorn in the side of England's King Edward I (opposite page). Edward had taken control of Scotland; Wallace raised an army of commoners that harassed the English forces. Wallace was captured and tried by the English (this is considered the first trial for war crimes); found guilty, he was put to death in London.

as Stoics for their belief that men's actions should be guided by logic, not passion, taught that the vanquished should be spared. At times, when a Roman general received the surrender of a town, instead of destroying the town and enslaving its population he became that town's ruler.

By the Middle Ages, the powerful Roman Catholic church attempted to limit wars between neighboring feudal lords to as few days as possible. A treaty that was called the Peace of God, which first evolved in France around A.D. 975, was one of the first attempts to protect the human rights of poor and unarmed Christian people in Europe. This treaty, which was extended at the Council of Clermont in 1095 by Pope Urban II to apply to Christians throughout the world, protected certain types of people—women, priests, merchants, and pilgrims—and their property from attack.

The Peace of God was followed in 1027 by the Truce of God, which prohibited fighting from 9 P.M. Saturday to 3 A.M. Monday. Eventually, the Truce of God was expanded to prevent fighting from Wednesday evening until Monday morning as well as during many church festivals, allowing about 80 days, scattered throughout the year, when warfare was permitted.

Violators of these two Christian provisions were excommunicated (expelled from the church community)—a harsh and effective punishment, as the church taught that the souls of nonmembers were doomed to hell for eternity.

During this time, different rules were applied to

wars between Christian nations than to wars between Christians and non-Christians, such as the series of wars against the Muslims in the Holy Land (1095–1291) that are known as the Crusades. The Crusades were extremely bloody and brutal, and neither side showed mercy. When the city of Jerusalem was captured by a Crusading army under Godfrey of Bouillon, at least 10,000 Muslim and Jewish "infidels" were slaughtered. Conversely, thousands of young Europeans were enslaved by the Muslims after the failed Children's Crusade of 1212.

The first trial for war crimes, historians believe, occurred in 1305 with the trial of William Wallace, a Scottish patriot. Wallace actually was tried for treason by the English king, but he contended that his actions in leading a Scottish uprising against England could not be treasonous because he had never sworn allegiance to the king, Edward I. His trial

marks the first time that judicial procedure was used to punish someone for breaking the law of war.

The struggle between England and Scotland had its roots in the death of Scotland's King Alexander III in 1286, followed by the drowning of Alexander's infant granddaughter and legitimate heir, Margaret, Maid of Norway, four years later. Their deaths embroiled Scotland in a war between two disputants for the crown. Seizing the opportunity, England's King Edward invaded the neighboring country in 1296, imprisoned the Scottish leader John of Balliol, and crowned himself king of Scotland.

In 1297, Wallace formed an army of commoners and defeated the English at Stirling Castle. Soon, much of Scotland was under his control, and he led his army into northern England. Wallace was defeated by Edward's force at Falkirk in 1298; though he continued fighting for several years, he was never able to marshal aid either from the Scottish noblemen or from the French, whom he had hoped to enlist as allies against England. In 1305 he was captured and taken to London for trial. Wallace was accused of waging a war of extermination against the people of northern England, "sparing neither age nor sex, monk nor nun." English jurists found him guilty, and Wallace was executed.

In the 17th and 18th centuries, humanist philosophy affected the way that wars were conducted and the rules for treatment of prisoners. The French jurist and political philosopher Charles Montesquieu (1689–1755) argued that killing prisoners of war is contrary to international law. Jean Jacques Rousseau (1712–1778) wrote that prisoners of war should be kept in healthy conditions, rather than dungeons, and should be freed at the end of the war.

In 1864 at Geneva, Switzerland, 16 European countries signed an international treaty intended to mitigate the horrors of war. This first Geneva convention provided that sick and wounded soldiers should be cared for, and that medical personnel, buildings, and transport could not be attacked. This was followed in 1906 by a second Geneva convention that extended the protections of the first convention to maritime warfare. At the same time, the two Hague conferences were held, and the agreements made there codified into international law.

A third Geneva convention was held in 1929, as a result of World War I, and required nations to provide information about prisoners of war and to allow representatives of a neutral state to visit prison camps to make sure that prisoners were being treated humanely.

Another international agreement made after World War I was the Kellogg-Briand Pact, signed by 61 countries including the United States, Great Britain, Germany, France, Italy, and Japan. This treaty stated that international disputes must be solved without resorting to use of force. However, there were a number of exceptions that made the Kellogg-Briand Pact ineffective, and the treaty did not provide any punishment for nations that violated its provisions. The Kellogg-Briand Pact proved to be powerless to stop the Japanese invasion of Manchuria in 1931, Italy's 1935 attack on Ethiopia, or Germany's aggression against Czechoslovakia and Poland—all events that led to World War II.

After the Second World War, as stories began to circulate about the atrocities committed by both the

Members of the League of Nations in session at Geneva, Switzerland, in 1929. The organization had been founded after World War I to "promote international cooperation and to achieve peace and security." Although the League of Nations was a failure, it served as a model for the United Nations, which was established after the Second World War to serve a similar purpose.

Nazi and the Japanese regimes against civilians and prisoners, a fourth Geneva convention was held in which the treaties underwent detailed revision. The 1949 convention provided special protection for the wounded, children under 15, women, and the elderly. Discrimination against prisoners of war or civilians in captured territories was forbidden on racial, religious, national, or political grounds, and prisoners were to be treated humanely. The treaty also prohibited torture, the punishment of a group of people for the actions of others, reprisals, and the forced use of civilians in an occupier's armed forces.

The nations that have signed the Geneva Conventions—and most countries in the world have—cannot withdraw from the agreement during wartime. Most importantly, the 1949 convention was extended to cover "armed conflict not of an international character," making this international agreement applicable to civil wars. This is an important provision, for under international law it allows nations to intervene in cases where atrocities are being committed against a portion of the population, such as in the case of Kosovo.

Today, all nations agree that because the rules of war are part of a larger international law, war crimes can be punished both by the state—for example, the government of a country where a camp commander orders prisoners to be tortured is responsible for punishing that commander—and by other nations, including the enemy.

During the most famous war crimes trials, the 1946 Nuremberg Trials of Nazi officials and the trials of top Japanese leaders that were held in Tokyo in 1948, prosecutors attempted to prove that four types of international law violations had been committed:

1. Crimes Against Peace: planning, preparing, initiating, or waging a war of aggression. To start a war of aggression (a war in violation of international treaties, agreements, or assurances, and for the sole purpose of conquest) "is not

only an international crime; it is the supreme international crime," stated the International Military Tribunal at Nuremberg.

2. Participation in a common plan or conspiracy to commit crimes against peace.

3. War Crimes: violations of the laws of war, including murder, ill-treatment or deportation to slave labor or for any other purpose of civilian populations of or in occupied territory; murder or ill-treatment of prisoners of war or persons on the seas; killing of hostages; plunder of public or private property; and wanton destruction of cities, towns, or villages, or devastation not justified by military necessity.

4. Crimes Against Humanity: murder, extermination, enslavement, deportation and other inhumane acts committed against any civilian population, before or during the war, or persecutions on political, racial, or religious grounds, whether or not in violation of the domestic law of the country where perpetrated.

Probably the best-known of war crimes trials are the ones held in Nuremberg, for it was there that the world gained a firsthand look at the brutal "Final Solution" that the Nazi government attempted to impose on the Jews of Europe—the Holocaust.

THE HOLOCAUST AND THE NUREMBERG TRIALS

On the night of October 27, 1938, Zindel Grynszpan and his family were rousted out of their beds and driven out of their home into a freezing rain by German police. In the streets were many of Grynszpan's neighbors, whom police herded into boxcars. Their crime? Grynszpan and the others were guilty of being Jewish, and Nazi policy was to expel all Jews who did not possess German citizenship. Zindel Grynszpan and thousands of other Jews were sent east to Poland in a campaign of forced emigration.

In Paris, Grynszpan's 17-year-old son Hershel heard the news and decided to gain revenge for all Jews. On November 7, 1938, Hershel Grynszpan went to the German Embassy and fatally wounded a diplomat named Ernst von Rath.

The response by the Nazis was swift and brutal.

Jewish inmates in the Nazi concentration camp at Buchenwald, 1945.

Organized by Reinhard Heydrich, one of the leaders of the Gestapo (Germany's secret police force), violent demonstrations against Jews broke out all over Germany. Jewish families were arrested and sent to work camps. Gangs of Nazi terrorists roamed the streets, breaking into and desecrating Jewish synagogues, burning homes, and looting shops. In fact, the streets were so covered by shattered shards from house and shop windows that the night of November 9, 1938, was labeled the night of broken glass, *Kristallnacht*.

The death of von Rath was a convenient excuse for the Nazis, allowing them to justify mass action against the Jews. There is no doubt that the leader of Germany, Adolf Hitler, gave permission for this awful revenge to take place. From the time Hitler rose to power in 1933, Jews had been encouraged to leave Germany. By 1938 more than half of Germany's Jewish citizens had departed, leaving behind their shops, homes, possessions, jobs, friends, and family members. Those who stayed had to endure abuse and humiliation, as hatred of Jews became a major theme of Nazi propaganda.

With the outbreak of war in September of 1939, another two million Jews in occupied Poland came under German control, while at the same time emigration to the outside world had become almost impossible. In Poland the Nazis grouped all Jews into ghettos, or confined areas within a city, where they could be controlled. The Jews in the ghettos were cut off from the outside world and not given enough food, which allowed slow starvation to reduce the population. The more able-bodied Jews were used as slave labor. Living conditions in the ghettos were harsh. Hard labor, overcrowding, and starvation were the dominant features of life. Police units guarding the ghettos had orders to shoot any Jew who ignored warnings to stay away from the fences that surrounded the ghetto.

By the middle of 1941, about 30,000 Jews had perished in street massacres and labor camps, and another

The assassination of German diplomat Ernst von Rath in November 1938 led to violent reprisals against Jews in Germany. The night of November 9, 1938, became known as Kristallnacht, *the night of broken glass, because of the damage to Jewish-owned shops such as the one pictured here.*

20,000 had died of starvation in the Polish ghettos. With the invasion of Russia that began on June 22, 1941, however, a new policy was implemented to systematically destroy entire Jewish communities. The Waffen SS (*Schutzstaffel*), an elite military unit charged with state security, had created special groups of soldiers known as *Einsatzgruppen*, or special killing forces. Their job was to eliminate as many Jews as possible in the hundreds of small towns and villages throughout the conquered territories on the Eastern Front. These groups organized local collaborators in Lithuania and

Heinrich Himmler (left), the head of the SS, and Adolf Hitler review a parade of German troops. Together, these Nazi leaders directed the Final Solution—Hitler's plan to eliminate all the Jews of Europe.

the Ukraine into murder gangs to help carry out this policy of extermination. Jews and other enemies of the state were lined up in front of trenches, shot, and covered with lime. Then another line of people would be shot. Local populations were encouraged to turn against the Jewish communities and destroy them.

By the end the year, though, it was evident to Nazi leaders that the mass shootings were not the most efficient method to eliminate whole populations. Shootings were slow and hard to keep secret. SS chief

Heinrich Himmler ordered his sections to find a more efficient way to execute large numbers of people. The new method they came up with involved filling closed trucks with Jews, then pumping the trucks full of poison gas. The dead were buried away from population centers, in sites where there were few witnesses.

The year 1942 saw the creation of a vast system to implement Adolf Hitler's "Final Solution"—complete extermination of the Jewish people—across Europe. Trains began to roll from East and West, bringing Jews to death camps in Poland. As the Jews from Germany and Eastern Europe were eliminated, the Nazis looked elsewhere for Jewish victims. Adolf Eichmann, head of the Gestapo's Jewish Affairs Section, directed his officers to round up Jews from France, Belgium, and the Netherlands and transport them to the death camps. In France, the deportation of foreign Jews was accomplished very quickly with the cooperation of the French police. France had a long history of anti-Semitism and French occupation leaders had already begun their own anti-Jewish program in 1940. In occupied Yugoslavia, Jews and Gypsies were murdered by firing squads.

In July 1941, Hermann Göring, second in the Nazi hierarchy only to Hitler, had sent the following message to SS officer Reinhard Heydrich, director of the Reich Main Security Office:

> I hereby commission you to carry out all necessary preparations with regard to organizational, substantive and financial viewpoints for a total solution of the Jewish question in the German sphere of influence in Europe.
>
> I further commission you to submit to me promptly an overall plan showing the preliminary organizational, substantive and financial measures for the execution of the intended final solution of the Jewish question.

Six months later, Heydrich outlined the steps the Nazis would take. Because the murder of Jews within sight of local German populations sometimes provoked opposition and was difficult for troops to carry out, it had been decided that areas of Eastern Europe that were controlled by the Nazis would be more appropriate sites to carry out the Final Solution. Heydrich also stated:

> In the course of the final solution, the Jews should be brought under appropriate direction in a suitable manner to the east for labor utilization. Separated by sex, the Jews capable of work will be led into these areas in large labor columns to build roads, whereby doubtless a large part will fall away through natural reduction. The residual final remainder which doubtless constitutes the toughest element, will have to be dealt with appropriately, since it represents a natural selection which upon liberation is to be regarded as a germ cell of a new Jewish development.

The unspoken truth was that those unsuited for road building—the elderly, children, many women, and the handicapped—would be eliminated immediately. It was also clear that the methods the *Einsatzgruppen* had already used to kill 1.4 million in the East would not be adequate to deal with 11 million more people. Shooting was too messy and the carbon monoxide gas trucks had proven too slow. Other methods needed to be developed to make the Final Solution easier and more efficient. Gas chambers seemed the best answer.

The results of the Final Solution are gruesome. By the end of the Second World War, the Nazis had murdered more than 5.8 million Jews—more than one-third of the world Jewish population. Under Hitler, the Nazis had committed mass murder, enslaved a portion of their population and used them as forced labor, tortured civilians and prisoners of war, and left Europe in a state of total destruction. The Nazis had brought death and destruction to 35 million people in Europe. The Nazis' victims cried for justice, and the victors wished to give it to them.

The intent to formally punish the Nazis for their crimes started long before World War II was over. In January of 1942, the governments-in-exile of nine

countries issued a statement of intent to punish all those responsible for crimes against their civilian populations. Later in 1942, as the Allied nations heard rumors of the Nazi death camps, the United States and Great Britain issued a declaration which expressed their resolve to punish those responsible for the policy of extermination against the Jews. At the Teheran Conference in 1943, U.S. President Franklin D. Roosevelt, British Prime Minister Winston Churchill, and Soviet Premier Joseph Stalin, declared their intention to punish Axis leaders for serious war crimes. Later in 1943, the foreign ministers of the United States, Great Britain, and the Soviet Union, meeting in Moscow, issued a warning that those guilty of atrocities, massacres, or executions would be sent back for judgment

Jews are forced out of the burning Warsaw ghetto in Poland by Nazi troops. They probably were taken to concentration camps, where they were forced into slave labor or murdered. This photo was exhibited as evidence during the trials of Nazi war criminals held in Nuremberg after the war.

Some of the important Nazi war criminals tried at Nuremberg. Each man is identified by name, and the sentence he received at the trial is listed.

and punishment to the countries in which they had committed their crimes.

After the war, representatives of the United States, Great Britain, and the Soviet Union met in London and issued a charter to create an International Military Tribunal to try the major Nazi war criminals. Obviously, the top-ranking Nazi officials, guilty of planning and carrying out Hitler's Final Solution, had to be tried and punished. But many of them would never stand trial. Hitler had committed suicide in the final days of the war. The head of the SS, Heinrich Himmler, and Hitler's minister of propaganda, Joseph Goebbels, were also dead. Reinhard Heydrich had been killed by an assassin's bomb. Of the top Nazi leaders, only Reichmarshall Hermann Göring had been captured.

Göring had been one of Germany's great World War I heroes, the last commander of the famed Richthofen Flying Circus fighter squadron once led by the Red

Baron, and he held the highest war decoration in Germany. Göring met Hitler in 1921 and joined the Nazi party soon afterward. When the Nazis gained power in 1933 Göring was given the task of creating the *Luftwaffe,* or German Air Force. A brilliant executive, Göring was later given the job of creating Germany's secret police, the Gestapo. The job of the Gestapo was to eliminate those who did not agree with Nazi aims. To aid this job Göring had developed a system of concentration camps during the 1930s. After the invasion of Russia in 1941 Göring was put in charge of the economic exploitation of Russia. He was reported as saying, "Naturally this giant area would have to be pacified as quickly as possible. The best solution would be to shoot anybody who looked sideways."

Early in the war Göring had been Hitler's designated successor. As the end drew near Göring made a move to take control of the Reich, so that he could surrender to the Allies, but he was arrested at Hitler's order. Thus, Göring found himself first a prisoner of the SS and later a prisoner of the Allies after Germany's surrender.

In addition to Göring, the International Military Tribunal indicted 23 other Nazi leaders, charging conspiracy, crimes against peace, war crimes, and crimes against humanity. The defendants included Rudolf Hess, a charter member of the Nazi party and third in line to succeed Hitler, who had been captured by the British early in the war; Heydrich's replacement, Ernst Kaltenbrunner, who was responsible for the extermination of millions of European Jews; German Foreign Minister Joachim von Ribbentrop; Wilhelm Keitel, the chief of the German Armed Forces High Command; Karl Dönitz, the commander in chief of the German Navy; Alfred Jodl, chief of staff of the German Army; and Hans Frank, the sadistic governor-general of Poland who had been responsible for the deportation and liquidation of nearly the entire Jewish population of that country. Each of the defendants was entitled to an attorney and was allowed to testify on his own behalf.

The trial, which was held in the town of Nuremberg in southern Germany, opened on November 20, 1945, and lasted for 10 months. Presiding over the trial were four distinguished judges: Lord Justice Geoffrey Lawrence of Great Britain, who was named president of the tribunal; Francis Biddle of the United States; Henri Donnedieu de Vabres of France; and Major General Johann Nikitchenko of the Soviet Union. The prosecuting teams were headed by Justice Robert H. Jackson of the United States, Sir David Maxwell-Fyfe of Great Britain, Charles Dubost of France, and Colonel Yuri Podrovsky of the Soviet Union. After the charges were read, each of the defendants stood in turn and declared their innocence.

On the second day of the trial Justice Jackson opened for the prosecution by saying:

> The privilege of opening the first trial in history for crimes against the peace of the world imposes a grave responsibility. The wrongs which we seek to condemn and punish have been so calculated, so malignant, and so devastating, that civilization cannot tolerate their being ignored because it cannot survive their being repeated. That four great nations, flushed with victory and stung with injury, stay the hand of vengeance and voluntarily submit their captive enemies to the judgment of the law is one of the most significant tributes that Power has ever paid to Reason.

In preparing the charges against the Nazi defendants, the prosecutors had used hundreds of thousands of documents that recorded every aspect of the operation of Hitler's Third Reich. These German archives revealed the murder of millions of innocent people. (During the trial some four thousand of these records were placed in evidence.) The Germans' own records, said Justice Jackson, would convict them.

During the trial new rules were established condemning crimes against humanity, for the actions of Nazi Germany had created a new problem. Among the crimes against humanity revealed at Nuremberg was the killing of civilians, the extermination of social, racial, and religious groups, the use of slave labor, the

Anne Frank

The story of Anne Frank, a teenage Jewish girl living in the Netherlands when Germany invaded and occupied the small country during World War II, is typical of many Holocaust victims. Anne, her family, and some friends went into hiding in a tiny room in an office building, with the help of non-Jewish workers from her father's company. Anne and the other seven Jews remained in their hiding place for more than two years.

In August of 1944 their hiding place was discovered by the Gestapo, and the eight Jews were sent to concentration camps. Anne died of typhus in the infamous Bergen-Belsen death camp in April 1945—just days before the camp was liberated by Allied troops. Anne's father, Otto Frank, was the only one of those hidden in the secret annex who survived the concentration camps.

Anne's story became known after Otto Frank returned to the Netherlands and visited the room in which he had spent two terrifying years. There, he found a diary that Anne, who hoped one day to become a famous writer, had kept. He edited

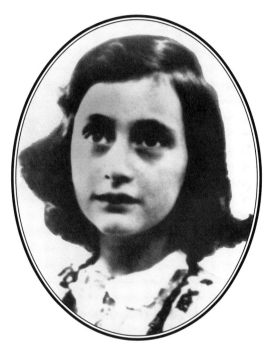

A photo of Anne Frank taken from her diary. "This is a photo as I would wish myself to look all the time. Then I would maybe have a chance to come to Hollywood," she wrote.

the material and submitted it for publication. *The Diary of a Young Girl,* in which the teen writes about her own growth, her family relationships, the experience of hiding, and events around her and her reaction to them, was first published in 1947. Since then, it has sold nearly 20 million copies, and Anne Frank has become a worldwide symbol of the millions of victims of the Holocaust.

forced deportation of peoples, the plundering of con-quered countries, and other inhumane acts. These crimes were not isolated incidents, but a series of delib-erate policies officially adopted by a world-recognized government and executed by agencies of that govern-ment in a systematic fashion. The results of the Nurem-berg court demonstrated that the political leaders who created the genocide would be held responsible for their crimes. Previously, only those who had shot hostages and civilians, and turned on the gas in the chambers had been punished.

At Nuremberg it was shown that the elimination of world Jewry was fundamental to Hitler's program and philosophy. In his book *Mein Kampf*, Hitler had written that the Jews were the enemy of mankind, and in his Reichstag speech of January 30, 1939, the Nazi leader had promised the "annihilation of the Jewish race in Europe." In his testimony at Nuremberg, Nazi Foreign Minister Joachim von Ribbentrop testified that at a meeting on April 17, 1943, Hitler had stated, "that the Jews must either be exterminated or taken to concen-tration camps." Under Nazi rule, Germany had been awash in anti-Semitic propaganda from such people as defendant Julius Streicher, who in his newspaper *Der Stuermer* had called for "the extermination of the peo-ple whose father is the devil." The Nazi Minister of Propaganda, Joseph Goebbels, was perhaps the most extreme advocate of Jewish persecution in the Nazi government. The commandant of the Auschwitz death camp, Rudolf Hoess, explained that Himmler's orders to exterminate thousands of Jews, "fitted in with all that had been preached to me for years."

In their defense, the Germans called witnesses to try and help mitigate the guilt of the defendants. But, under skillful cross-examination by the prosecutors, most witnesses turned out to be more damaging than helpful. The basic attitude of the defendants was that the International Military Tribunal had no right to try

them at all, but they did attempt to work within the framework of the trial. The Nazis based their defense on three claims:

1. Hitler and others were to blame for everything.
2. The men on trial had no knowledge of the crimes that were committed.
3. The laws by which they were being tried were ex post facto, or established after the fact. (in other words, the Germans had broken no laws because the laws did not exist until after their actions came to light.)

During the trial Göring was the prime defendant. He set the tone and provided the leadership for the defendants. At one point Göring testified for three days about the Nazi regime and denied that he was responsible for war crimes, crimes against humanity, and wars

Two American soldiers make a gruesome discovery as they look into the ovens at a liberated concentration camp. Because the murder of millions of Jews, Gypsies, Roman Catholics, dissidents, and others had been part of a deliberate policy of the Nazi government, the German leaders were held responsible for these crimes against humanity, even though they had not actually pulled the triggers or turned the switches in the gas chambers.

of aggression. During his presentation for the defense Göring declared that he knew nothing about the mass murder of Jews and others, but this was easily disproved.

In the course of the trial, dozens of witnesses were called, thousands of documents were accepted by the courts, and five million words were recorded. When final judgment was delivered, 10 of the defendants were sentenced to death by hanging, seven more were given prison sentences, and only three were acquitted. The judges also ruled that the leadership corps of the Nazi Party, the SS, the Gestapo, and two other organizations of the Nazi regime, were criminal. This meant that individual members of those organizations could be tried for any crimes they had committed. Of those condemned to death, only Hermann Göring was able to cheat the hangman. Just two hours before he was to have been hanged he committed suicide by swallowing a capsule of poison in his cell.

For prosecutor Whitney R. Harris, the Nuremberg experience represented a step forward in the evolution of international law. "For the first time in history, the judicial process was brought to bear against those who had offended the conscience of humanity by committing acts of military aggression and related crimes," he later wrote. "No man would deny that what was done by Hitler and his associates . . . was morally wrong. Nuremberg represented the transition of these wrongs from the moral to the legal plane. Crimes against humanity and initiating and waging of aggressive war, are now judicial concepts."

The Allies held additional trials against people holding senior positions in the Nazi regime. Twelve major trials were held in Nuremberg by American military judges up to the middle of 1949. These trials included those of doctors in the euthanasia program; the manager of the war armaments program; Nazi judges; members of the SS Economic Administrative Office, which was responsible for running the concentration camps; industrialists who had exploited slave labor and plundered foreign property; military generals, for the shooting of hostages; members of the SS Office for Reich and Resettlement Matters, the Office of Reich Commissar for Strengthening the German Race, and the Lebensborn Organization on charges of taking part in the annihilation of Poles and Jews and deporting racially unsuitable children from the occupied territories to Germany; state ministers, for war crimes and crimes against humanity in their sphere of influence; and senior officers of the German armed forces.

The British, French, and Soviets also held tribunals in their zones of occupation to punish Nazi war criminals. In addition, Belgium, Denmark, Luxembourg, the Netherlands, Norway, Poland, Yugoslavia, Czechoslovakia, the Federal Republic of Germany, and others held trials in their own states.

Even with this massive roundup, thousands of Nazi war criminals escaped justice, with many settling in friendly countries and living under assumed identities. The United States government protected talented scientists and engineers, and many of them came to the United States to help develop the U.S. rocket program in the 1950s and 1960s. Only about 20 percent of the estimated 200,000 Nazi war criminals were ever put on trial. Millions of others who had helped to bring about the Final Solution escaped punishment.

THE JAPANESE WAR CRIMES TRIALS

In the war with Japan, the evidence of wartime atrocities was indisputable. But this was not the same as in Germany, where Hitler and the agents of his government had conspired in torture and mass murder. In Asia, individual soldiers and their officers had committed acts of unspeakable barbarity and it was for this that they were punished in a series of war crimes trials. The main focus of justice was on those responsible for four major horrors, the Rape of Nanking, the Bataan Death March, the Thailand-Burma Railroad POWs, and the Sack of Manila.

The major victims of Japanese war atrocities were China and her people. China and Japan officially went

Hideki Tojo, in the left-center of the photo, is sworn in during his trial by the Tokyo War Crimes Tribunal. Tojo, the former prime minister and military leader of Japan, had ordered the bombing of Pearl Harbor and run the Japanese war effort until July 1944. Tojo was convicted of crimes against humanity and hanged on December 23, 1948.

to war in July 1937 and they fought until the last Japanese surrendered in September 1945. In December 1937, the Japanese army had overrun the capital of the Republic of China, located in the ancient city of Nanking. In a six-week period the Japanese looted and burned the city and systematically raped, tortured, and murdered thousands of Chinese civilians. Japanese soldiers arrested thousands of young men, marched them to the city's outskirts, then killed them with machine guns and bayonets or doused them with gasoline and burned them alive. From there the Japanese soldiers moved throughout the city looting private homes. Women were raped and subjected to horrible tortures, and defenseless civilians were murdered. As bad as things were in Nanking, they might have been much worse if not for the intervention of the international community in Nanking—including Nazi officials and businessmen living in the city, who insisted that the atrocities end. Despite this, after the war it was estimated that more than 260,000 Chinese civilians and surrendered soldiers died at the hands of Japanese soldiers in Nanking.

The brunt of the blame for the Nanking atrocities fell on General Iwane Matsui, the commander of Japan's Central China Expeditionary Force. Matsui served as the most obvious target: on December 17, 1937, he had entered the city with great pomp and ceremony, perched on a chestnut horse, as his soldiers cheered him on. The evidence at his trial in Tokyo showed that he made an attempt to stop the barbarity but was unsuccessful. The Japanese then tried to cover up the atrocities despite the wide coverage in world newspapers. The Japanese emperor, and civilians in the cabinet, claimed that they knew nothing about the event until the war was over. As the senior Japanese commander on the scene, Matsui was blamed for the Rape of Nanking.

After the war several Japanese leaders were tried in

Nanking for war crimes. The trial of Lieutenant General Hisao Tani, commander of the Japanese 6th Division, created a sensation in Nanking. According to the indictment, Tani's men had been responsible for hundreds of stabbings, burnings, drownings, strangulations, and rapes, as well as thefts and destruction. More than 80 witnesses testified to these horrors at the trial. Just over one month after the trial began, the court found Tani guilty, and pronounced this sentence: "Hisao Tani, having been convicted of instigating, inspiring and encouraging during the war the men under his command to stage general massacres of prisoners of war and non-combatants and to perpetrate such crimes as rape, plunder and wanton destruction of property is hereby sentenced to death." On April 26, 1947, Hisao

Thousands of American soldiers died during the Bataan Death March, a forced 70-mile march to a prison camp. Mistreatment of prisoners of war was a central issue in war crimes trials involving the Japanese: 27 percent of the 132,000 Allied soldiers in Japanese custody died in prison camps.

Tani was put to death by a firing squad.

The first war crimes trials in Asia had been held a year and a half earlier, in Manila, the capital of the Philippine Islands. The main defendants were General Tomoyuki Yamashita, who was indicted for sacking the city during the war, and General Masaharu Homma, who was charged with atrocities that occurred in 1942 while the Japanese marched 37,000 prisoners of war for 70 miles across the Bataan peninsula to a concentration camp. Thousands died during the Bataan Death March, as it came to be known.

As the Japanese retreated from American troops during the invasion of the Philippines in 1944–45, they waged a systematic campaign of brutality, terrorism, and murder against the population of the Philippines. Thousands of Filipinos, including women, children, infants, the elderly, the sick, priests, and nuns, fell victim to Japanese soldiers. Property damage in the Philippines was tremendous and Manila itself was looted and burned. When Yamashita, the commanding general, surrendered to American forces in September 1945, he was charged as a war criminal and arraigned on October 8. His trial commenced three weeks later. The indictment against him charged:

> between 9 October 1944 and 2 September 1945, at Manila and at other places in the Philippine Islands, while commander of armed forces of Japan at war with the United States of America and its Allies, unlawfully disregarded and failed to discharge his duty as commander to control the operations of the members of his command, permitting them to commit brutal atrocities and other high crimes against people of the United States and of its allies and dependencies, particularly the Philippines, and he, General Tomoyuki Yamashita, thereby violated the laws of war.

The five-member military commission found Yamashita guilty, even though the evidence against him was weak, and sentenced him to hang. This trial

set a precedent that military commanders could be held accountable for the actions of their soldiers, if those actions constituted war crimes or crimes against humanity.

The trial of General Homma, who had been commander in chief of Japanese forces in the Philippines from December 1941 to August 1942, opened in late December 1945. Again, the legal issue was the responsibility of the commander. Charges against Homma included ordering the bombing of Manila after it was declared an open city, as well as the infamous Bataan Death March. He was also charged with violating the

Japanese lieutenant general Masaharu Homma awaits sentence. Homma was accused of ordering the bombing of Manila after it had been declared an open city, ordering the Bataan Death March, and violating the Geneva Conventions by mistreating prisoners of war. General Homma was sentenced to death by firing squad.

Geneva convention by mistreating prisoners of war. Through evidence, the testimony of witnesses, and a partial admission by the accused, prosecutors established that Homma had known about some of the violations at the time they occurred. In February 1946, the military commission found Homma guilty of failure to "control the operations of the members of his command and permitting them to commit brutal atrocities and other high crimes." For these crimes, Homma faced a firing squad.

While the trials in Nanking and Manila were significant, the most famous Japanese war crimes trials were held in Tokyo by the International Military Tribunal for the Far East. The Tribunal sentenced 25 major war criminals, especially those responsible for planning the war, to a variety of punishments. Seven, including former prime ministers Hideki Tojo and Koki Hirota, were hanged.

The Tokyo War Crimes Trial began in the capital of Japan in May 1946 and lasted for 18 months. The trial drew more than 200,000 spectators and 419 witnesses, and the transcript of the trial spanned over 48,000 pages, contained 10 million words, and included 799 affidavits and depositions and 4,336 exhibits.

The treatment of prisoners of war by the Japanese received close examination during the Tokyo trials. Japanese prison camp administrators had tried to get the maximum amount of work from the prisoners with the minimum cost in food and supplies. In the opinion of the prosecutors, the POW camps were centers of crime that turned the Japanese into murderers. Of the 50,000 prisoners who were forced to work on the construction of a railway that connected Thailand and Burma, 16,000 died from a combination of torture, disease, and starvation. Japanese documents shown at the trial stated that useless prisoners were to be killed. Other evidence that was revealed during the trial showed that Japanese medical officers removed hearts and livers from healthy prisoners, and that cannibalism of prisoners was allowed when other food was not available. On the whole, the Japanese record of treating prisoners of war was much worse than that of the Nazis: Only 4 percent of the 235,000 English and American POWs held by Germany and Italy during the war died, compared to 27 percent of the 132,000 in Japanese custody.

Overall, relatively few Japanese were tried and convicted for wartime atrocities. Most of the defendants and 210,000 government officials were allowed to return to private life and were simply banned from further activity in public office. However, the Allied war crimes trials in the East, along with those in Nuremberg, served a purpose: firmly establishing the judicial right, under international law, to prosecute those guilty of crimes against humanity.

THE
TRIAL OF
ADOLF
EICHMANN

O n Monday May 23, 1960, the prime minister of Israel, David Ben-Gurion, told the Israeli Parliament that Adolf Eichmann, former head of the Nazi Gestapo's Jewish Affairs section, had been seized in Argentina and was in Israeli custody. Eichmann, as a Nazi department head, was accused of being responsible for organizing the arrest and transportation of millions of Jews, Gypsies, and others to their deaths in concentration camps.

Eichmann's capture was due, for the most part, to a 16-year tracking effort by famed Nazi hunter Simon Wiesenthal. Born December 31, 1908, in what was then the Austro-Hungarian Empire, Wiesenthal survived twelve Nazi concentration camps before United States troops freed him from a camp in Austria. After World War II, Wiesenthal dedicated his life to documenting the atrocities of Hitler's regime and hunting Nazi war criminals from his base in Vienna, Austria. The capture of Eichmann, one of the architects of the

This rather ordinary-looking man was in fact one of the most infamous mass murderers in history. As head of the Gestapo's Jewish Affairs Section, Adolf Eichmann ordered the arrests of Jews, organized their deportation to concentration camps, and authorized the killing of millions.

Holocaust, was Wiesenthal's most spectacular success.

Eichmann seemed to be a normal, socially adjusted person, but his willingness to become totally absorbed in his work and to follow orders allowed him to direct the murders of six million Jews. According to Wiesenthal, "he would have had six million Gypsies gassed if there had been that many. Or six million left-handers. If Hitler had commanded him not to kill the Jews but to ship them to Palestine he would have done that quite as well."

♠   ♠   ♠

At the end of World War II in Germany, investigators first went after people who had humiliated, beat up, and shot people dead in front of witnesses. People who ran the establishment, such as Eichmann, were slower to be identified. The first list of war criminals published by the Jewish Agency identified him only by his last name. With more investigation, Eichmann's importance began slowly emerging. It was clear that deportation orders had come from him, and that he was the principal person responsible for all of the extermination machinery. Eventually he was placed on the list of wanted Austrians. For Simon Wiesenthal the search for Eichmann became more important than anything else he had done.

The Austrian leaders of the Third Reich had agreed that they should meet in the Austrian Alps after the war was over, so Eichmann dutifully went there. His wife had moved to the town of Altaussee in the same region and he wanted to see her anyway. It was confirmed that he was seen in the town on May 4, 1945, by a former member of his staff. Eichmann's wife, Frau Veronika Liebl Eichmann, and her three children, Klaus, Dieter, and Horst had moved to Altaussee in April.

At the end of 1947 Frau Eichmann applied to the district court in Ischl, Austria, to have her husband declared dead. According to Wiesenthal "thousands of women whose husbands had not returned needed a declaration of death to collect pensions for themselves and their children, and in order to marry again. The courts handled these matters as routine." But if Eichmann was declared dead any official search for him would come to an end. Wiesenthal explained to the court that this "dead" person was an important Nazi war criminal and the application for declaration of death was denied.

Eichmann was hiding in American internment camps where he would be less conspicuous than hiding in some lonely house. He moved through at least three camps in Austria, German Bavaria, and along the Rhine River. Eichmann, and others, may have recovered boxes of "dental gold"—gold fillings that had been taken from Jews murdered in the concentration camps—that had been buried in a pasture near Altaussee, and used this money to finance their escape from Germany. Wiesenthal was convinced that a Croatian committee helped Eichmann get to Rome by 1950, where he obtained a passport, which he needed for a South American visa. Both Brazil and Argentina were favorite destinations for the Nazis. In Juan Peron's Argentina especially, the former Nazis exercised considerable power. They helped organize the Argentine army as well as the country's industrial sector, and their money was welcomed in Argentine banks without questions about where it had come from. Eichmann could feel secure in Argentina.

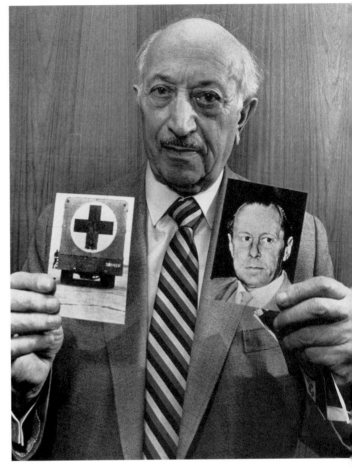

After surviving the Holocaust, Simon Wiesenthal dedicated his life to hunting down Nazi leaders and bringing them to justice. He is shown here with the photo of a wanted German war criminal. Wiesenthal considered finding Eichmann his greatest achievement.

Eichmann's Argentinian papers show the name he adopted upon escaping from occupied Germany, Ricardo Klement. After he was identified as the wanted war criminal, members of the Israeli security agency Mossad kidnapped Eichmann and brought him to Israel for trial.

In 1951, Frau Eichmann and her sons disappeared from the house in Altaussee. She had taken the children out of school in the middle of the term without a leaving certificate, meaning they would not be accepted at any German or Austrian school. The house was left furnished and the rent continued to be paid but Frau Eichmann did not return. Wiesenthal thought she probably had left for South America.

In April of 1959 Adolf Eichmann's mother died in Germany. There was a big notice in the newspaper that listed the mourning relatives, including the name Vera Eichmann. Wherever Veronika Liebl was living, she had adopted the name "Eichmann" again. Wiesenthal questioned Veronika's mother, who stated she was living in South America with a new husband. The Israelis were able to verify the name of the husband as Ricardo Klement. Wiesenthal thought that this must be Adolf Eichmann. So now Wiesenthal suspected that Eichmann and his wife and sons were living in Buenos Aires. But Wiesenthal needed a way to verify that Klement was Eichmann. His chance came in 1960 when Eichmann's father died and this death notice was signed by his daughter-in-law, Vera Eichmann.

The only picture of Adolf Eichmann known to exist had been taken in 1934. Wiesenthal desperately needed a more modern photograph to confirm that Ricardo Klement was Adolf Eichmann. Wiesenthal sent two photographers to the funeral hoping that Adolf Eichmann might attend, but only Eichmann's brothers Emil, Robert, Otto, and Friederich attended. Wiesenthal's photographers got pictures of all four brothers. Otto Eichmann had looked very much like his brother Adolf when they were younger so Wiesenthal decided to use his new photograph of Otto to track down Adolf. The Israeli authorities were notified about Wiesenthal's suspicions and soon two young Israelis came and took Wiesenthal's photos and other information.

In 1960, the Mossad, Israel's secret service, found and tracked Eichmann to a house on Garibaldi Street in Buenos Aires. In a daring international kidnapping, the Israeli agents abducted Eichmann and brought him to Israel.

The Eichmann trial opened in Jerusalem less than a year later. It was a public trial—broadcast live on radio, photographed, and recorded for posterity. Many survivors of the Holocaust testified duing the course of the trial, relating personal stories of Nazi atrocities. The entire population of Israel and much of the world, was focused on the trial as the whole Nazi mechanism of extermination was revealed, almost for the first time.

For his own protection, Eichmann sat in a glass booth with a translator headset wrapped around his head. In his defense his lawyers claimed that he was only following orders, but it was clear what a large role he had played in the Holocaust. However, the defense raised several arguments. First, that the Jewish judges

Protected by a bulletproof glass cage, Adolf Eichmann stands during his trial. The prosecution produced more than 100 witnesses and 1,600 documents to prove Eichmann's role in carrying out Hitler's Final Solution. The court rejected Eichmann's claim that he was "just following orders," indicating that there is a moral obligation to reject orders that constitute a crime against humanity.

would not give Eichmann a fair trial; second, that Eichmann had been kidnapped and not legally transferred to Israel for trial; third, that the law under which Eichmann was being prosecuted had been created after the fact of the crimes he was alleged to have committed, and was therefore unjust; and fourth, that all the crimes had been committed outside the state of Israel and before its establishment, and that therefore an Israeli court could not have jurisdiction. After all of these arguments were rejected by the judges, Eichmann pleaded "not guilty" to the charges of crimes against the Jewish people, crimes against humanity, and war crimes.

To present its case, the prosecution used more than 100 witnesses and 1,600 documents, many bearing Eichmann's signature. The prosecution showed the persecution of the Jews in Nazi Europe and the personal involvement of Eichmann, through the Gestapo office for Jewish affairs, in helping to carry out Hitler's Final Solution. The defense did not deny these facts, but claimed that Eichmann was merely a minor staff member who had no choice but to carry out the orders of his superiors.

The Israeli court rejected Eichmann's arguments and agreed with the prosecution that Eichmann had fully embraced the disagreeable tasks involved in his job. On December 15, 1961, he was found guilty on all counts. After confirmation of the verdict by the Israeli

Supreme Court and the refusal of Israel's president to grant a pardon, Eichmann was sentenced to death. The court had found, "The fact that any person acted pursuant to the order of the Government or a superior does not free him from his responsibility for a crime, but may be considered in mitigation."

On May 31, 1962, Adolf Eichmann was put to death by hanging. This execution is the only death sentence the state of Israel has ever carried out. In this important trial, which aroused great interest, the grim story of the Holocaust was revealed for all the world to see. The trial led to an increased interest in Holocaust research and spurred other investigations and trials. It also indicated that "just following orders" is no defense when it comes to crimes against humanity.

The Banality of Evil

Hanna Arendt, a German-born Jew who had left her homeland in 1933 when the Nazis came to power, attended the trial of Adolf Eichmann. In her controversial 1963 book *Eichmann in Jerusalem,* she coined the phrase "the banality of evil" to discuss Eichmann's defense. Eichmann did not come up with the idea for the Final Solution; he was simply following orders unquestioningly, and doing what his society told him was his duty, Arendt wrote. Rather than being "radically evil," meaning that his actions came consciously from some depth of evil in his spirit or soul, she described the Nazi official's evil as "thoughtless" or "banal" (meaning "commonplace") in that he did not really think about what he was doing or understand that it was wrong.

"Eichmann did not hate Jews," Arendt cautioned. "And that made it worse, to have no feelings. To make Eichmann appear a monster renders him less dangerous than he was. If you kill a monster you can go to bed and sleep, for there aren't many of them. But if Eichmann was normality, then this is a far more dangerous situation."

She also wrote:

It is indeed my opinion now that evil is never "radical," that it is only extreme, and that it possesses neither depth nor any demonic dimension. It can overgrow and lay waste the whole world precisely because it spreads like a fungus on the surface. It is "thought-defying," as I said, because thought tries to reach some depth, to go to the roots, and the moment it concerns itself with evil, it is frustrated because there is nothing. That is its "banality." Only the good has depth and can be radical.

GENOCIDE

The word *genocide* was coined in 1944 by Raphael Lemkin to mean the destruction of a nation or an ethnic group. It is formed from the ancient Greek words *genos*, for race or tribe, and *cide*, for killing. In the 20th century, more than 60 million people have been victims of genocide.

The Holocaust of Nazi Germany is the most well-known instance of an attempt to destroy an entire race, but genocide is not a new phenomenon. The razing of cities and the slaughter of people who were "different" were common in ancient times. The Crusades that pitted Christians against Muslims in the Holy Land often contained episodes of slaughter; not only were members

---

A Rwandan soldier looks at the hundreds of skulls and remains of victims of genocide at a memorial in Bisesero, Rwanda. In the 20th century, more than 60 million people have been victims of genocide, which is defined as the deliberate and systematic destruction of a racial, political, or cultural group.

of one religion targeted by the other for destruction, but the noncombatant Jews who lived in the Holy Land also were attacked. Jews were often blamed for everything that went wrong, including the Black Plague that swept across Europe during the Middle Ages.

Wars between Catholics and Protestants in Europe included the Saint Bartholomew's Day massacre of thousands of French Huguenots (a Protestant political faction in that country) in 1572, and the devastation of Europe during the Thirty Years War. After the discovery of the New World, and throughout the period of colonization by the major European powers of the 16th, 17th, and 18th centuries, native peoples were often massacred or enslaved by the European invaders, especially the Spanish, English, and Portuguese. After the United States of America won its freedom from England in 1783, attempts to wipe out Native Americans and their culture marred the young nation's westward expansion.

In the 20th century, a number of genocidal actions have taken place. A coldly calculated effort at genocide occurred during the First World War, when the Muslim government of Turkey conducted a campaign of extermination against that country's Christian Armenian residents. In February 1915 Turkish soldiers began to systematically massacre hundreds of thousands of Armenians.

The first step was to disarm the many Armenian soldiers in the Turkish army, followed by the disarming of Armenian citizens. Then, Turkish political clubs such as the Young Turks inflamed the public with tales about Armenian treachery and atrocity. Next, the Armenian leaders and all those with wealth and influence were arrested and deported. This was followed by the general deportation of all Armenians. Their destination was the mountains and deserts of Mesopotamia and Syria. To non-Turkish witnesses, these deportations were little more than death caravans. One witness was the Italian

consul-general in the city of Trebizond in Turkey, who was personally shaken by the scenes of genocide:

> The passing of gangs of Armenian exiles beneath the windows and before the door of the Consulate; their prayers for help, when neither I nor any other could do anything to answer them; the city in a state of siege, guarded at every point by 15,000 troops in complete war equipment, by thousands of police agents, by bands of volunteers and by the members of the "Committee of Union and Progress"; the [cries], the tears, the abandonment's, the many suicides, the sudden deaths from sheer terror, the [burnings], the shooting of victims, the ruthless searches through the houses and in the countryside; the hundreds of corpses found every day along the exile road; the young women converted by force to Islam or exiled like the rest; the children torn away from their families or from the Christian schools, and handed over by force to

The bodies of Armenians massacred by the Turks in 1915. Although countries such as the United States, Great Britain, France, and Russia condemned the atrocities, no actions were taken against the Turkish rulers who organized and directed the slaughter.

Muslim families, or else placed by hundreds on board ships with nothing but their shirts, and then capsized and drowned in the Black Sea and the river. These are my last memories of Trebizond which still torment my soul and almost drive me frantic.

Those that arrived in the desolate relocation areas faced slow death by exposure and starvation. To Henry Morgenthau, the American ambassador to Turkey, the deportations seemed merely to be a cover for genocide. According to Morgenthau, "When the Turkish authorities gave the orders for these deportations they were merely giving the death warrant to a whole race; they understood this well, and in their conversations with me, they made no particular attempt to conceal the fact."

Despite Turkish attempts to hide the death and destruction from the rest of the world, horror stories of Armenian massacres quickly became known. Henry Morgenthau reported that:

Though all sorts of impediments were placed on traveling, certain Armenians, chiefly missionaries, succeeded in getting through. For hours they would sit in my office and, with tears streaming down their faces, they would tell me of the horrors through which they had passed. Many of these, both men and women, were almost broken in health from the scenes which they had witnessed. In many cases they brought me letters from American consuls, confirming the most dreadful of their narrations and adding many unprintable details.

On May 24, 1915, the governments of France, Great Britain, and Russia issued a declaration denouncing the massacres of the Armenian population as "crimes against humanity and civilization for which all members of the Turkish government will be held responsible together with its agents implicated in the massacres."

Unfortunately, for the Armenians there was little real justice. The treaties that ended the First World War imposed on Turkey the obligation to ensure free and equal treatment for racial and religious minorities and to return the remaining deportees to their homes. Some of those involved in the massacres were tried, but not punished. A free and independent state of Armenia was proposed but only a small Soviet republic was actually created. The Turkish government claimed that it was only relocating the Armenian people for their own protection, and denied any genocidal intent, but the statistics show a different picture. From a pre-war population of 1.8 million, close to one million Armenians disappeared. These people were killed by soldiers, died by the roadside, died of starvation and sickness, or died from conditions in the relocation camps.

Hitler was very much aware of the Armenian genocide, and learned a lesson about the post–World War I world's seeming lack of concern. While the Armenian genocide had been widely condemned by the Allies during the war, afterward there was no attempt to punish those responsible for the extermination of a million people. It seemed that countries could kill off their minority populations and get away with it.

The German genocide against the Jews followed this same pattern. The exterminations were coordinated between the bureaucracies of the German state, the Nazi party, the military, and big business. The German genocide of the Jews, Gypsies, and others became a massive operation of systematic murder. In the words of author Leo Kuper:

> Who would have believed that human beings would send out mobile killing units for the slaughter of unarmed men, women and children in distant lands? Or that they were capable of organizing, on the model of a modern industrial plant, killing centers which processed their victims for slaughter, as if on a conveyor belt; eliminating waste, gathering in, with careful inventory, their few possessions, their clothes, gold teeth, women's hair, and regulated the distribution of these relics? Or that the killing centers would be combined with slave camps, in which the exploitation of labor was carried to the extreme of

Several Hutu children sit next to a corpse in a refugee camp in Zaire. The children fled from Burundi when the Tutsi-controlled government there instituted a policy to rid Burundi of Hutus in 1972.

rapid expendability, or that . . . leading German firms such as I. G. Farben and Krupp would establish branches in the vicinity of the gas chambers and crematoria?

Following the atrocities of World War II, the problem of the prevention and punishment of genocide was taken up by the United Nations General Assembly at the end of the war. On December 11, 1945, the Assembly passed a resolution which defined genocide as "a denial of the right of existence of entire human groups, as homicide is the denial of the right to live of individual human beings." The General Assembly then affirmed "that genocide is a crime under international law which the civilized world condemns, and for the commission of which principals and accomplices—

whether private individuals, public officials or states-
men, and whether the crime is committed on religious,
racial, political or any other grounds—are punishable."

On December 9, 1948, the General Assembly of
the United Nations approved the Convention on Prevention and Punishment of the Crime of Genocide
which defined the crime of genocide as follows:

> In the present Convention, genocide means any of the
> following acts committed with intent to destroy, in whole
> or in part, any national, ethnic, racial, or religious group,
> as such:
> (a) Killing members of the group;
> (b) Causing serious bodily or mental harm to members of
> the group;
> (c) Deliberately inflicting on the group conditions of life
> calculated to bring about its physical destruction in
> whole or in part;
> (d) Imposing measures intended to prevent births within
> the group;
> (e) Forcibly transferring children of the group to another
> group.

The legislation was adopted after much discussion
about whether the elimination of political dissidents
constituted genocide. The representative of the Soviet
Union argued that "the inclusion of political groups
was not in conformity with the scientific definition of
genocide and would . . . distort the perspective in
which crimes should be viewed." The French representative countered with the view that while "in the past,
crimes of genocide had been committed on racial or
religious grounds, it was clear that in the future they
would be committed mainly on political grounds." The
United States feared that the Convention would not be
passed if political genocide was included and took a
position of exclusion. Therefore, the U.N. Convention
does not include violence against groups of people who
are politically opposed to their nation's government.
This loophole in the convention has been used by
national governments to justify mass murders of minor-

ity populations. For example, the government of Burundi argued that it was putting down a political insurrection and maintaining public order to justify its genocidal massacre of 100,000 minority Hutu tribesmen in the 1970s.

In general, it has been impossible to separate the political aspects of civil disputes from racial, national, or religious issues. Many genocides have focused on minority or dissident groups with political objectives. The well-known Russian author Alexander Solzhenitsyn has been especially critical of the crimes of the regime of Joseph Stalin. Solzhenitsyn reported that 15 million peasants (called *kulaks*) were evicted from their farms and died of starvation in a massive resettlement program conducted during 1929 and 1930. During 1937 and 1938 Stalin annihilated rival communist leaders and restless members of minority ethnic groups alike. According to Solzhenitsyn, Stalin's enemies were "all sentenced together and driven off in herds to the slaughterhouses of the [Gulag] Archipelago." At the end of the Second World War returning Russian prisoners and other "corrupted" Soviet citizens were sent to the Siberian work camps. Needless to say, these exiles died in droves. The official grounds for deportation were betrayal of the fatherland and assistance to the Germans.

Other examples occurred in Indonesia and Cambodia, where political opponents of the government were targets for slaughter. In October 1965, an attempted coup was stopped in Indonesia. The communist party was accused of plotting to overthrow the government and in the resulting struggle for power between the army and the communists over 200,000 party members were killed. Likewise, in 1979 a subcommittee of the Commission on Human Rights of the United Nations reported that the revolutionary forces of the communist Khmer Rouge government of Cambodia had acted harshly to quell dissidents. The cruel and despotic

Russian author Alexander Solzhenitsyn was a harsh critic of the Soviet regime of Josef Stalin. Himself a sur-vivor of eight years in Russ-ian prison camps, his works, such as One Day in the Life of Ivan Denisovich *(1963) and* The Gulag Archipelago *(1974), depict the brutal conditions of the camps.*

Khmer Rouge regime, under the direction of general secretary Pol Pot, executed political opponents, intel-lectuals, and even ordinary persons whose attitudes toward the government had not been deemed satisfac-tory. Even members of the communist Soviet Union described Cambodia as a vast concentration camp, where rivers of blood flowed and a ruthless policy of genocide was being carried out. After Vietnamese forces invaded Cambodia in January 1979, forcing Pol Pot and the other Khmer Rouge leaders to relinquish power and flee the capital, the Soviet Union defended the invasion by bringing charges of genocide against the Khmer Rouge government before the Security Council of the United Nations.

A more recent example occurred during the mid-1990s in the African nation of Rwanda, where between 500,000 and one million people were killed between April and June 1994. An ethnic group known as the Hutu, who supported the existing government of Rwanda, began indiscriminately attacking Rwandan members of another ethnic group, the Tutsi, that supported a new, Democratic government. Hundreds of thousands of Tutsis fled the country to the Republic of the Congo (formerly Zaire). The massacres in Rwanda certainly were motivated in part by ethnic hatred, but political issues also played a role.

Application of the U.N. Convention on Prevention and Punishment of the Crime of Genocide has been difficult. In March 1974, the International League for the Rights of Man charged the government of Paraguay with complicity in the crime of genocide against the Guayaki Indians. The charge to the United Nations Secretary General included the enslavement, torture, and killing of Indians on reservations in Paraguay, and the withholding of food and medicine which resulted in deaths from starvation and disease. Other charges included massacres outside the reservation, the splitting up of families, the sale of young girls into prostitution, and the denial of the Guayaki language and culture. The government of Paraguay responded by denying an intentional campaign to eradicate the natives. "Although there are victims and victimizer, there is not the third element necessary to establish the crime of genocide—that is intent," said Paraguay's Minister of Defense. "Therefore, as there is no intent there is no genocide." As a result, Paraguay's government was never convicted of crimes against humanity. Other 1970s cases in which the question of intent determined the outcome included the government of Brazil's treatment of the Indians of the Amazon Basin, and the actions of U.S. servicemen in Vietnam.

The provision of the Convention that created the greatest outcry was its proposal to establish an international court that would investigate and judge charges of genocide. Many countries, including the United States, thought that an international criminal justice system would infringe on the sovereignty of individual nations. As a result, strong enforcement powers were not written into the Convention.

However, without an international criminal justice system there is no way to realistically punish those who order genocide to be carried out. In many cases, the government is ultimately responsible for attacks on its minority populations, and will not impose punishment. As a result, it has been very difficult to establish government responsibility for genocidal massacres. In Bosnia and Kosovo, genocidal massacres have been denied by the Serbian government; the Serbs also continue to harbor numerous perpetrators who have been indicted by the International Tribunal in The Hague, Netherlands. Without enforcement powers, the Genocide Convention of the United Nations has not been an effective instrument in the prevention and punishment of crimes against humanity and genocide.

♠   ♠   ♠

Discussing the Armenian massacre in 1915, Ambassador Morgenthau commented, "Technically of course, I had no right to interfere. According to the cold-blooded legalities of the situation, the treatment of Turkish subjects by the Turkish government was purely a domestic affair." However, as a result of the Allied war crimes operations at Nuremberg and in the East, the judicial right to prosecute those guilty of

As violence erupted in Rwanda in 1994, tens of thousands of people left the country to avoid being victims of the government-supported genocide.

crimes against humanity is now firmly established in international law. What is not clear is the right to intervene to prevent crimes against humanity or genocide within the borders of a sovereign nation, such as the NATO intervention in Kosovo on humanitarian grounds in 1999.

At its founding, the charter of the United Nations included provisions for the suppression of war, crimes against humanity, and genocide. Based on the experiences of the first fifty years of the twentieth century, these ideals were central to the reason why the United Nations exists. In practice, however, the performance of the United Nations in the suppression of crimes against humanity and genocide has been less than ideal. In general, the United Nations and other sovereign states stand by and watch the unfolding of genocidal conflict, and do little more than provide humanitarian relief for the refugees. The ideal of sovereignty, combined with the complementary idea of noninterference in the domestic affairs of a state, stands in the way of effective action against "domestic" genocide.

INTERNATIONAL CRIMINAL TRIBUNALS

etween July 1997 and October 1999, North Atlantic Treaty Organization (NATO) forces captured four suspected war criminals and killed a fifth in a gunfight in Bosnia. By the end of 1999, some 24 indicted war criminals were in international custody and two had been sentenced; other trials were underway at the International Criminal Tribunal in The Hague, Netherlands, that was investigating atrocities in the former Yugoslavia.

But the most important war criminals remained free. Radovan Karadzic, the former president of the Bosnian Serbs, is one of the most wanted men in the

Survivors of the massacre at the Bosnian town of Srebrenica protest the continued freedom of Radovan Karadzic, the former president of the Bosnian Serbs, and his military commander Ratko Mladic. When Bosnian Serb forces overran the town in 1995, they massacred some 8,000 Bosnian Muslims. Although the instigators of the Bosnian fighting have been indicted for war crimes, they remain free and have never been brought to trial.

Jean-Paul Akayesu, the former mayor of Taba in central Rwanda, arrives in handcuffs for his 1997 trial for genocide in Tanzania. Akayesu was found guilty by the International Criminal Tribunal for Rwanda, becoming the first person to be convicted for genocide.

world. Western officials have little doubt that Karadzic masterminded the policy of "ethnic cleansing" that resulted in the murder, imprisonment, or expulsion of more than a million Bosnian Muslims between 1992 and 1994. Karadzic and his military commander, Ratko Mladic, were indicted in 1995 on 36 counts of crimes against humanity, stemming mostly from the siege of Sarajevo and the slaughter of civilians in the designated "safe area" of Srebrenica. This indicted war criminal would be arrested if he ever left the Serbian-held section of Bosnia. However, he continues to be protected by the Serb government.

The harshness and incredible nature of intense ethnic hatred and the divisions which develop are difficult for Americans to comprehend. In the former Yugoslavia, a geographic region of great cultural diversity, no one culture holds a majority and cross-cultural marriages have been quite common. Often, only an individual's last name serves to identify him or her as a member of a particular minority. Throughout the history of this region, however, ethnic tensions have existed. The categorical distinctions are strict, and the roots of the present ethnic divisions can be traced back more than 600 years to the Battle of Kosovo, where the invading Ottoman Turks defeated the Serbs and created a Muslim ruling class over Christian majorities. The struggles of separate peoples tenuously linked together as one nation show few signs of ceasing, particularly because the ethnic tensions have created the present civil and international conflict.

Genocidal conflict is by no means limited to Europe. In 1994, when Hutu death squads entered the African community of Taba in central Rwanda, they convinced the Hutu mayor, Jean-Paul Akayesu, to assist them in their genocide efforts. According to testimony at his genocide trial in Tanzania, Akayesu turned into one of Rwanda's most notorious executioners. Akayesu was charged with organizing the killing of more than 2,000 men, women, children, and unborn fetuses. The genocide was part of a three-month period of mass killings sparked by the death of Rwandan President Juvenal Habyarimana when his plane was shot down by rocket fire over the capital Kigali in April 1994. Roughly one million Tutsi and some moderate Hutu were killed and 300,000 became homeless refugees.

In September of 1998, three judges of the United Nations International Criminal Tribunal for Rwanda meeting in Arusha, Tanzania, found ex-mayor Akayesu guilty on nine counts of genocide, torture, rape, murder, and crimes against humanity, and acquitted him on six other charges. Akayesu had pleaded not guilty to all 15 counts and has appealed the verdict, but meanwhile he faces a maximum sentence of life imprisonment. Akayesu became the first defendant ever to be convicted of the crime of genocide by an international court in a case that sets legal precedents which are also binding on the U.N.'s war crimes tribunal in the Hague.

Since the end of the Cold War there has been an increase in atrocities and crimes against humanity. The United Nations and the international community has slowly been taking on the responsibility for justice through the use of temporary international criminal tribunals. Tribunals have been created by the United Nations Security Council to prosecute offenders in Rwanda and in the former Yugoslavia, which hopefully will go a long way toward establishing an international rule of law that offending national governments and their leaders cannot escape from.

The establishment of the Tribunal of Criminal Justice by the United Nations Security Council is reminiscent of the trials at Nuremberg and Tokyo, and recalls the 1947 version of the "new world order" which incorporated a "return to fundamental principles" of international law. These principles included applying international law to the goal of achieving justice defined by morality, recognizing the rights of individuals under international law, removing the defense of official state action from the application of international law to the conduct of individuals, limiting a nation's sovereignty in accordance with the demands of international law, and making even private citizens responsible for violations of international law. After 1947, these principles began to be incorporated into many treaties, publications, and judicial decisions in such a way that they were becoming customary international law.

The International War Crimes Tribunal in the Netherlands is piecing together evidence to bring to justice those responsible for the worst atrocities committed in the former Yugoslavia. By 1995, indictments had been brought against 52 persons, ranging from detention camp commanders to Bosnian Serb president Karadzic and his top general Mladic. Of the defendants, forty-five are Serbs; seven are Croats. Investigations of other Bosnians are in the works. While much of the evidence is circumstantial, it is damning and plentiful. Thousands of pages of documents compiled by United Nations investigators show that the brutalities of the war in Bosnia and Croatia were not the work of roving, blood-crazed lunatics but, rather, the result of an orchestrated campaign executed by the Yugoslav National Army and paramilitary thugs operating in coordination with it. Serbian paramilitary units have been blamed for the slaughter, rape, and suffering of thousands of non-Serbian men, women, and children in Croatia and Bosnia. This systematic slaughter and "ethnic cleansing" continued in the Serbian province of Kosovo. These forces could not have carried on their carnage without the sponsorship of Slobodan Milosevic, Serbia's president.

In many ways, the war in Bosnia was Milosevic's creation. As the Yugoslav federation began to collapse, the Serbian president lit the fuse by stridently backing the right of Serbs living in Croatia and Bosnia to join a "Greater Serbia." Milosevic skillfully developed and deployed the tools he needed to make his nationalist vision a reality. These were the Yugoslav Army and the paramilitary units that attached themselves to it. The Army and its commanders coordinated their assaults with paramilitary groups, as well as with local militia and police forces. Together, these groups engineered not just the conquest of land but executions, rapes, and the displacement of thousands of innocent civilians.

The judges of the Yugoslav tribunal have delivered several decisions that strengthen the jurisprudence of international humanitarian law. The distinction between a civil and an interstate war had long been significant in international law. The Yugoslav tribunal has

Dusan Tadic, a Bosnian Serb accused of crimes against humanity that occurred in Bosnia during 1992, was the first person to be tried for war crimes since the Nuremberg and Tokyo tribunals of the 1940s. However, many of the charges against Tadic were dropped when judges ruled that the fighting in Bosnia had been an internal conflict, and thus he could not be tried for war crimes.

weakened this distinction considerably. The judges determined that the tribunal has jurisdiction over crimes against humanity and war crimes whether they occur in an internal or an international armed conflict. In fact, the judges confirmed that customary international law no longer requires any connection between crimes against humanity and armed conflict of any character. Indictment for genocide, the most extreme crime against humanity, has never required the existence of an armed conflict.

However, in the Yugoslav tribunal's first trial, most of the charges against Bosnian Serb defendant Dusko Tadic were dismissed when the judges, in a surprise ruling, said the war was an internal one. War-crimes charges apply only to an international conflict. If the fighting is deemed internal, prosecutors could pursue charges of genocide or crimes against humanity, which are more difficult to prove because the prosecution must establish specific intent. The NATO intervention in Kosovo was based upon the fact that crimes against humanity were being committed against the ethnic Albanians by the Serbian government.

The Bosnian war and the slowness of reaction to it serve as a reminder that violence in the form of genocide and warfare cannot be stopped in the courtroom. The procedures of a court, and the lack of enforceability of its judgments outside of the actions of the U.N. and goodwill of the nations who are parties to it, do not meet the need for swift action when the issue is not only the placing of blame for acts of genocide, but the prevention of such ongoing acts. The United Nations Genocide Convention refers to both prevention and punishment, but while international courts consider who should be accused, tried, and punished, they have been ineffective in the more immediate and more important work of preventing genocide.

PREVENTING CRIMES AGAINST HUMANITY

imor is one of hundreds of small islands in the South Pacific Ocean. It is part of the Malay Archipelago, which also encompasses Malaysia, the Philippines, and Indonesia.

In the 15th and 16th centuries, the islands of the Malay Archipelago were called the East Indies by explorers and traders from Europe. The first Europeans to reach these islands and establish settlements were the Portuguese. For more than 300 years, the people of Timor were ruled by Portugal, which had an empire of colonies that spanned the globe. The Portuguese controlled the eastern half of the island; the western half was ruled by another colonial power, the Dutch. After World War II, the one-time Dutch colonies, including West Timor, received their independence, becoming the nation of Indonesia. East Timor, however, remained

After the people of East Timor voted overwhelmingly for independence from Indonesia in 1999, violence broke out on the small island.

a Portuguese holding until 1974, when that country finally withdrew its control of the island.

In 1975, the Indonesian government offered to annex East Timor, but the people refused. With popular support, the independent Democratic Republic of East Timor was declared on November 28. Nine days later, the Indonesian military invaded East Timor.

Thousands of East Timorese were killed in the fighting that followed, while tens of thousands died of starvation or disease in internment camps, where they had been placed while the Indonesian army tried to eliminate resistance. On the day of the invasion, Australian journalists picked up a radio message from East Timor: "The Indonesian forces are killing indiscriminately. Women and children are being shot in the streets. We are all going to be killed. . . . This is an appeal for international help. Please do something to stop this. . . ."

East Timor was declared part of Indonesia, despite the protests of the United Nations. Between 1975 and 1999, it is estimated that more than 200,000 East Timorese were killed by the Indonesian forces that occupied the country.

In 1998, the longtime president of Indonesia, General Suharto, resigned. His successor, B. J. Habibie, opened the door to independence for East Timor by inviting the country to vote either to remain a province of Indonesia or to become independent. Ninety-nine percent of the people of East Timor turned out for the election in August 1999, and 75 percent voted for independence.

Unfortunately, after this vote Indonesian-supported paramilitary organizations started a wave of violence that soon swept across the tiny island. Habibie declared martial law in East Timor, sending in the Indonesian army (called the TNI), but the soldiers merely looked the other way while the paramilitaries continued terrorizing the population. The atrocities included massacres, rapes, destruction of homes and villages, and looting.

Tens of thousands fled from East Timor to West Timor or to neighboring countries like Australia. The accounts of refugees, like this one told by a 17-year-old high-school student, are chilling:

> The truck slowed down. . . . so I sat up and looked through the slats of the truck. I saw the most terrible thing that will stay in my memory forever. I saw a man being executed. He was a Timorese man. . . . His back was facing me and I could see that his hands were tied. He was naked and being pulled backwards by a piece of wire toward a flagpole. When he arrived at the flagpole, I saw his head being cut off with a machete or sword. I saw his head fall off onto the ground. I could not see the person who cut off his head because my vision was obstructed by one of the TNI's legs. It was outside the Aitarak militia headquarters. I saw the machete and then I saw the man's head fall off. I did not see any other adults. I only saw children with the Indonesian flag tied onto their heads. When I saw this I screamed to my mother, 'Mummy! Mummy! They cut off his head!' The military in the truck did not react in any way.

In response, a United Nations peacekeeping force, led by Australian troops, landed in Dili, the capital city of East Timor. The U.N. force attempted to quell the violence and bring order back to East Timor. On October 20, 1999, the Indonesian legislature ratified the East Timorese vote, allowing the country to become an independent nation. Unfortunately, East Timor is a country in disarray: between 300,000 and 600,000 citizens either were killed or fled the marauding militias.

In the nearly 25 years since General Suharto's invasion of East Timor, the United States, Great Britain, and Australia have been criticized for failing to take strong action against Indonesia. President Gerald Ford and his advisors apparently knew beforehand that the 1975 invasion that would take place, and Indonesia's military continued to receive both U.S. training and

Bishop Carlos Belo, East Timor's spiritual leader and a Nobel Prize winner, casts his ballot in the United Nations–organized vote on independence, August 30, 1999. The results of the vote sparked a new wave of violence, supported by the Indonesian army, on the troubled island.

weapons during and after the attack. Indonesia was a key ally for the United States in Southeast Asia, where American forces had recently withdrawn from Vietnam, and the U.S. government did not want to jeopardize that relationship.

The United States also helped prevent the United Nations from taking action to relieve the suffering of the East Timorese. As a member of the Security Council, the U.N. body that is responsible for maintaining international peace, the United States voted in 1975 for a resolution ordering Indonesia to withdraw from East Timor. The next year, however, the United States abstained from voting on a similar resolution. Between 1975 and 1982, eight General Assembly resolutions were presented supporting freedom for the East Timorese; the United States voted against seven.

U.S. policy toward East Timor started to change during the Clinton administration. The United States sponsored a U.N. resolution criticizing Indonesia for the killings in East Timor. And in September 1999 President Bill Clinton urged the United Nations to take an even greater role in preventing mass killings and crimes against humanity, such as those that have occurred in East Timor.

"When we are faced with the deliberate organized campaigns to murder whole peoples or expel them from their land, the care of victims is important, but not enough." Clinton said. "We should work to end the violence. . . . We need international forces with the training to fill the gap between local police and military peacekeepers.

"Sometimes collective military force is both appropriate and feasible," Clinton continued. "Sometimes concerted economic and political pressure combined with diplomacy is a better answer, as it was in making possible the introduction of forces into East Timor."

♠   ♠   ♠

It is essential and urgent that ways are found to prevent disputes. Clearly the world was unprepared for the genocidal slaughters of Bosnia and Rwanda, or the violence of Kosovo and East Timor. A Carnegie Commission Report titled *Preventing Deadly Conflict* published in 1997 concluded that the prevention of deadly conflict is too difficult for any one single institution or government. The Commission believes that war and mass violence are the result of deliberate political decisions, and that those decisions can be adjusted so that mass violence does not result. The key, according to the Commission, is "early, skillful, and integrated applications of political, diplomatic, economic, and military measures."

Most modern conflicts are wars within states rather than wars between states. These conflicts use modern weapons and rely on strategies of ethnic expulsion and annihilation. The strategies employed in these conflicts deliberately target women, children, the poor, and the weak. When long-standing grievances are exploited by political leaders, the scene is set for violence. The Carnegie Commission report identified three broad aims of preventive action.

First, prevent the emergence of violent conflict. This is done by creating capable states with representative governments based on the rule of law, with widely available economic opportunity, social safety nets, protection of fundamental human rights, and robust civil societies. The aim is to prevent dangerous circumstances from developing.

Second, prevent ongoing conflicts from spreading. This is done by creating political, economic, and, if necessary, military barriers to limit the spread of conflict within and between states. Firebreaks may be created through well-designed assertive efforts to deny the warring parties the ability to resupply arms, ammunition, and hard currency, combined with humanitarian operations that provide relief for innocent victims.

Third, prevent the reemergence of violence. This is done through the creation of a safe and secure environment in the aftermath of conflict and the achievement of a peace settlement. This environment can be established through the rapid introduction of security forces to separate enemies, oversee disarmament plans, and provide a stabilizing presence.

International commitment to the prevention of conflict is necessary for success. However, well-intentioned efforts, if not carefully planned, can make

matters worse. The Commission recommends that an international organization, country, or prominent individual needs to take charge of preventative efforts. This organization would then coordinate an integrated response to the situation and bring together all the governments, international organizations, nongovernment agencies, and private relief organizations with the local responsible leadership. The availability of resources is critical to defuse the developing crisis. The participation of community and national leaders in all aspects of the international response is necessary to reduce tension and allay fears regarding the motives of outside forces.

When crisis threatens, traditional diplomacy must continue but more urgent efforts will be needed to pressure conflicting parties to continue discussions and to facilitate a nonviolent resolution of the crisis. As the situation deteriorates, states should resist the traditional

A U.N. vehicle patrols a buffer zone on the island of Cyprus. Peacekeeping forces can create a safe and secure environment in the aftermath of conflict.

Economic sanctions and other measures can be used to help prevent crimes against humanity. Here, the United Nations Security Council is voting on a resolution that would lift harsh sanctions against Iraq if that country agrees to allow a U.N. team to inspect its weapons facilities.

urge to suspend diplomatic relations as a substitute for action and instead maintain open lines of communication with the leaders of the groups in crisis. Second, governments and international organizations must express the danger of a developing crisis in clear terms so that all people can understand. Third, the crisis should go before the United Nations Security Council, or the relevant international organization, early enough to permit preventative action. And fourth, quiet diplomacy and dialogue should be encouraged in the early stages of the crisis.

If stronger actions are needed, a number of economic measures are available to influence the conflicting parties. Economic sanctions can be used as a part of a broader strategy that puts political and economic pressure on the parties. Steps should be taken to reduce unwanted side effects and minimize the suffering of innocent civilians and the economic losses suffered by neighboring countries. The granting of political or economic benefits in exchange for policy adjustments could include favorable trade terms, tariff reductions, subsidies, or access to advanced technologies. A link between responsible, nonviolent behavior and the promise of greater rewards can be a potent tool.

Situations will also arise where diplomatic responses and economic measures are not enough to prevent the outbreak of deadly conflict. The Commission felt that in order to prevent deadly conflicts, organizations must be willing to apply forceful measures when necessary. These measures must be governed by universally accepted principles as required in the United Nations charter. The threat of force must be used as a measure of last resort. Lastly, the force must be part of an integrated strategy and used jointly with diplomatic, political, and economic measures.

Peacekeeping missions can help monitor and restrain tense situations. The conflicting parties should be clearly separated and must agree to a cease-fire and the presence of an outside force. Experience in a number of United Nations missions in Bosnia, Cambodia, Haiti, Rwanda, Somalia, and elsewhere suggests the need to plan carefully to execute responsible peacekeeping deployments. Law and order operations must be designed to establish and maintain legitimate local control.

One disadvantage of peacekeeping forces is that the stays may be lengthy, such as the deployment on the island of Cyprus that has separated Greek and Turkish factions since the 1960s.

In order to address the root causes of deadly conflict the Commission recommends peace-building activities that meet people's basic economic, social, cultural, and humanitarian needs, and rebuilds societies shattered by crisis. The three core needs of any society—security, justice, and an effort to ensure the well-being of the people—must be met. A system of law, consistent and fair police forces, an independent and impartial judicial system, and a penal system that is fair and prudent are also needed to ensure stability and reduce violence.

The Commission states that: "Major preventative action remains the responsibility of states, and especially their leaders. States must decide whether they do nothing, act alone, act in cooperation with others, or work with elements of the private sector. It should be an accepted principle that those with the greatest capacity to act have the greatest responsibility to do so."

The United Nations has been the traditional focal point to marshal the resources to prevent deadly conflict. One of the United Nations' challenges is how it can adapt its mechanisms to manage international disputes. The United Nations is fully dependent on its membership for the money and the people to carry out its mission. With the increasing number of conflicts within states, the international community must develop a new concept of national sovereignty and international responsibility. A major conflict in ideals still exists in respect to the rights of national sovereignty, and the prevention of slaughter within sovereign states, which will be difficult to resolve. Reform of the United Nations Security Council is needed to make it more representative of the membership and more legitimate in fulfilling its responsibilities.

Regional organizations, in the opinion of the Commission, should be strengthened for preventative purposes. A range of diplomatic, political, and economic measures for regional use should be developed to help prevent dangerous situations from exploding into violence. These organizations could provide an early warning of problem areas and work with the United Nations to support more assertive efforts to promote peace.

In the words of the Commission report: "Conflict, war and needless human suffering are as old as human history. In our time, however, the advanced technology of destruction . . . and the pressure of rapid population growth have added monstrous and unacceptable dimensions to the old horrors of human conflict. . . . The prevention of deadly conflict has a practical as well as moral value; where peace and cooperation prevail, so do security and prosperity."

Further Reading

Arendt, Hannah. *Eichmann in Jerusalem: A Report on the Banality of Evil.* New York: Viking, 1963.

Bauer, Yehuda. *A History of the Holocaust.* New York: Franklin Watts, 1982.

Black, Eric. "East Timor: An Inconsistent Case of U.S. Policy." *The Minneapolis Star Tribune,* 12 June 1999.

Bosch, William J. *Judgment on Nuremberg: American Attitudes Toward the Major German War Crimes Trial.* Chapel Hill: University of North Carolina Press, 1970.

Carnegie Commission on Preventing Deadly Conflict, *Preventing Deadly Conflict: Executive Summary of the Final Report* (Washington DC: Carnegie Commission on Preventing Deadly Conflict, 1997).

Chang, Iris. *The Rape of Nanking: The Forgotten Holocaust of World War II.* New York: Basic Books, 1997.

Churchill, Ward. *A Little Matter of Genocide: Holocaust and Denial in the Americas.* San Francisco: City Lights Books, 1998.

Conot, Robert E. *Justice at Nuremberg.* New York: Harper and Row, 1983.

Friedlander, Henry. *The Origins of Nazi Genocide: From Euthanasia to the Final Solution.* Chapel Hill: University of North Carolina Press, 1995.

Gilbert, Martin. *The Holocaust.* New York: Holt, Rinehart and Winston, 1985.

Harris, Whitney R. *Tyranny on Trial: The Evidence at Nuremberg.* Dallas: Southern Methodist University Press, 1954.

Hedges, Stephen J., and Peter Cary. "Will Justice Be Done?" *U.S. News & World Report* 119, no. 25 (25 December 1995): 44.

Hirsch, Herbert. *Genocide and the Politics of Memory: Studying Death to Preserve Life.* Chapel Hill: The University of North Carolina Press, 1995.

Isenberg, Beth Ann. "Genocide, rape, and crimes against humanity: an affirmation of individual accountability in the former Yugoslavia in the Karadzic actions." *Albany Law Review* 60, no. 3 (Spring 1997): 1051–79.

Johnson, Paul. *Modern Times: The World from the Twenties to the Nineties*. New York: Harper Perennial, 1991.

Kahn, Leo. *The Holocaust Years: Society on Trial*. New York: Bantam Books, 1981.

Kuper, Leo. *Genocide: Its Political Use in the Twentieth Century*. New Haven: Yale University Press, 1981.

Littell, Franklin H., Irene G. Shur, and Claude R. Foster Jr., eds. *The Holocaust: In Answer*. West Chester, Pa.: Sylvan Publishers, 1988.

Manchester, William. *American Caesar: Douglas MacArthur 1880–1964*. Boston: Little, Brown, 1978.

Marrus, Michael R. *The Holocaust in History*. Hanover, N.H.: University Press of New England, 1987.

Minear, Richard H. *Victors' Justice: The Tokyo War Crimes Trial*. Princeton, N.J.: Princeton University Press, 1971.

Piccigallo, Philip R. *The Japanese on Trial: Allied War Crimes Operations in the East, 1945–1951*. Austin: University of Texas Press, 1979.

Rückerl, Adalbert. *The Investigation of Nazi Crimes, 1945–1978*. Hamden, Conn.: Archon Books, 1980.

Scheffer, David J. "International Judicial Intervention" *Foreign Policy* 102 (Spring 1996): 34.

Shapiro, William E. ed. *The Twentieth Century: Trial at Nuremberg*. New York: Franklin Watts, 1967.

Shirer, William L. *The Rise and Fall of the Third Reich: A History of Nazi Germany*. New York: Simon and Schuster, 1960.

Whitelaw, Kevin and Richard J. Newman. "Time Is Running Out for Mr. Ethnic Cleansing, but the Case Against Karadzic May Be Weak." *U.S. News & World Report* 124, no. 14 (13 April 1998): 38.

Wiesenthal, Simon. *Justice Not Vengeance*. New York: Grove Weidenfeld, 1989.

Index

Index

Picture Credits

NEIL CHIPPENDALE is a Social Studies teacher at Octorara Area High School in Chester County, Pennsylvania. He has a bachelor's degree in history and a master's degree in education and information systems. Neil is continuing his graduate studies in history at West Chester University. *Crimes Against Humanity* is his first book.

AUSTIN SARAT is William Nelson Cromwell Professor of Jurisprudence and Political Science at Amherst College, where he also chairs the Department of Law, Jurisprudence and Social Thought. Professor Sarat is the author or editor of 23 books and numerous scholarly articles. Among his books are *Law's Violence, Sitting in Judgment: Sentencing the White Collar Criminal,* and *Justice and Injustice in Law and Legal Theory.* He has received many academic awards and held several prestigious fellowships. In addition, he is a nationally recognized teacher and educator whose teaching has been featured in the *New York Times,* on the *Today* show, and on National Public Radio's *Fresh Air.*